JESUS

JESUS

David Flusser

Translated by Ronald Walls

from German

HERDER AND HERDER

1969
HERDER AND HERDER NEW YORK
232 Madison Avenue, New York, N.Y. 10016

Original edition: *Jesus in Selbstzeugnissen und Bilddokumenten*
Hamburg, Rowohlt, 1968

Grateful acknowledgment is made for permission to reproduce the photographs in this volume: Alfred Bernheim, Jerusalem: 16, 45, 54, 60, 87, 92, 110, 118; Alliance Israélite Universelle: 113; Department of Antiquities and Museums, Ministry of Education and Culture, State of Israel: 6, 51, 55, 58, 59, 64, 74, 86, 97, 106, 117, 127; Department of Archaeology, Hebrew University of Jerusalem: 63, 79, 83, 109; Foto Sheridan: 107, 108, 112, 115, 121, 124, 125; Friedrich Wilhelm Kantzenbach, Kehl: 89 right; Historia Photo, Bad Sachsa: 89 left; H. Roger Viollet, Paris: 31, 104; *The Jesaja Manuscript and the Habakkuk Commentary, The Dead Sea Scrolls of St. Mark's Monastery,* vol. I, New Haven (the American School of Oriental Research), 1950, Plate XLIX: 37; *The New Testament, Views of the Biblical World,* vol. 5, Jerusalem (International Publishing Company): 12; Photo Orith, Jerusalem: 11, 15, 19, 21, 23, 26, 30, 33, 35, 49, 77, 85, 95, 111, 123, 132; Rowohlt Archives: 24, 27, 28, 39, 101, 128, 129.

Library of Congress Catalog Number 73–81781
© 1969 by Herder and Herder, Inc.
Manufactured in the United States

CONTENTS

The Pilate Stone. Found in Caesarea in 1961. The only inscription in which Pilate is mentioned. There he is designated: [PON]TIUS PILATUS [PRAE]FECTUS IUDAE[AE]. This stone confirms that Pilate was not procurator.

THE SOURCES

The main purpose of this book is to show that it is possible to write the story of Jesus' life. True, we have fuller records about the lives of contemporary emperors, and some of the Roman poets; but, with the exception of the historian Flavius Josephus, and possibly St. Paul, among the Jews of post Old Testament times Jesus is the one about whom we know most.

Every biography has its own peculiar problems. We can hardly expect to find information about Jesus in non-Christian documents. He shares this fate with Moses, Buddha, and Mohammed, who likewise received no mention in the reports of non-believers; and so, the only important Christian sources concerning Jesus are the four gospels: Matthew, Mark, Luke, and John. The rest of the New Testament tells us almost nothing about his life, and the fourth gospel is correctly regarded as biographically unreliable. The first three gospels are, in the main, based upon common historical material. Therefore, they can be printed in three columns to form a synopsis. Such a book is called a "synopsis"—hence the name "synoptic gospels" given to the first three books of the New Testament. Is, then, the absence of non-Christian documents an insuperable obstacle in the way of knowledge of the life of Christ?

When a religious genius appears within an environment that allows of precise documentation of his development, and of the circumstances of his life, there is always a temptation to try to uncover the psychological background leading up to this religious phenomenon. The reason why such psychological studies are often unsatisfactory is because the Spirit blows where he wills. This is especially true of personalities, themselves possessed by the Spirit. Who, for example, would dare to give a psychological analysis of the mystery of the personality of St. Francis? Our inability to provide a psychology of Jesus that would not sound a jarring note arises not from the type of sources at our

7

Genuine sources

disposal so much as from the nature of the personality of Jesus.

That is the way it is: even if objective documentation is plentiful, the most genuine sources concerning a charismatic personality are his own utterances, and the accounts of the faithful—read critically, of course. Thereafter the testimony of outsiders serves as a control. Let us take two modern examples. All that is significant about Joseph Smith (1805–44), founder of the Mormons, can only be learned from him, and from Mormon documents. Then there is the case of the African, Simon Kimbangu, who performed miracles of healing in the Belgian Congo from March 18 to September 14, 1921. He died in exile in 1950. Following the Christian model, his followers believed him to be the Son of God; but the documents do not make it clear what he thought of himself. Because of the brevity of his public activity, no unequivocal answer can be given to the question of his own self-assessment; and the testimony of the Belgian authorities in the Congo are as helpful in his case as are the archives of the governor Pilate, or the records in the chancellery of the high priest in the case of Jesus.

The early Christian accounts about Jesus are not as untrustworthy as people today often think. The first three gospels not only present a reasonably faithful picture of Jesus as a Jew of his own time, but consistently maintain his style of speaking of the Savior in the third person. An impartial reading of the three gospels results in a picture, not so much of a redeemer of mankind, as of a Jewish miracle-worker and preacher. There can be little doubt that this picture does not do full justice to the historical Jesus. Obviously such a picture did not require the Resurrection experience of the post-Easter Church before it could be portrayed. A series of miracle-legends and sermons certainly cannot be interpreted as a "kerygmatic" preaching of faith in the risen and glorified Lord, as most present-day scholars and theologians try to do. The only gospel that teaches a post-Easter Christology is the gospel according to St. John, and so it is of less historical value than the three synoptic gospels.

The Jesus portrayed in these gospels is, therefore, the histori-

*In the 3 Syn Gospels, the historical Jesus + the θ
kerygmatic X is presented.*

cal Jesus, not the "kerygmatic Christ." How is this to be explained? It is generally accepted that the main substance of the synoptic gospels comes from two sources: an old account of the life of Jesus which is reproduced in Mark, and a collection of *Sayings,* known and used along with the old account by Matthew and Luke. Both of these chief sources were produced in the primitive congregation at Jerusalem, and were translated into Greek. They contained the picture of Jesus as seen by the disciples who knew him. In addition, there was a certain amount of secondary material that came from the Jewish-Christian community. This had emerged out of dialogue—and later conflict— between Palestinian, and perhaps Syrian, congregations, and non-Christian Jewry. This material would seem to be reflected chiefly in the gospel according to St. Matthew.

For Jewish Christianity, even in later centuries when the Church in general regarded the view as heretical, Jesus the miracle-worker, teacher, prophet, and Messiah, was more important than the risen Lord of the kerygma. At a very early date, things had been different among the Hellenistic Christian congregations founded by Greek Jews, and composed predominantly of non-Jews. In these congregations, redemption through the crucified and risen Christ was the heart of preaching. It is no accident that the writings originating in these communities— for example the letters of St. Paul—scarcely mention the life and preaching of Jesus. It is perhaps a stroke of luck, as far as our knowledge of Jesus is concerned, that the synoptic gospels were written fairly late—apparently after 70 A.D.—when the mighty creative power within the Pauline congregations had died down. For the most part, this later stratum of the synoptic tradition found its first echo in the redactions of the separate evangelists. If we examine this material with an unprejudiced mind, we learn from the content and the manner of expression that it is concerned, not with kerygmatic statements, but with Christian platitudes.

The true facts are almost completely obscured, however, because in this century people have tended more and more to

9

identify the old account that lies behind Mark with our gospel according to St. Mark. There are serious scholars today, it is true, who have isolated the secondary editing of Mark; but as a rule, they refuse to draw the logical conclusions. If Mark's gospel is a thorough revision of the original material, it can scarcely be identical with the old account upon which it is based. We may assume, therefore, that this old account, and not the revision, was known to both Luke and Matthew. Upon these presuppositions, R. Lindsey (see Bibliography) has freshly examined the synoptic problem, and come to the following conclusions— which find support from other arguments too: Matthew and Luke, besides drawing upon the *Sayings,* also drew directly upon the old account; the editor of Mark used Luke for his version, and Matthew, besides using the old account, often drew upon Mark. It follows that when Matthew and Mark use almost the very same words it is Mark, and not the old account, that is reproduced in Matthew.

Even if we refuse to accept Lindsey's arguments, and regard Mark as the model used by Matthew and Luke, it is not so difficult for modern scholars to distinguish the work of editing from the original traditional material in the gospels. This is an important fruit yielded by the editorial-historical school, who seem to be gaining more and more supporters. The adherents of this school often seem to be quite unaware of the fact that they have opened up the way to sounder research into the life of Jesus. This study intends to make the conclusions of this school, and Lindsey's solution, bear fruit by unlocking both of these ancient sources: the old account and the *Sayings.* Thus, we shall often leave the separate gospels, and try to separate the original material from its editorial framework in all three gospels. In these cases, we will place the abbreviation "cf." before the first reference. The reader will be able to follow our method by using a synopsis. In order to understand Jesus, we have to know about contemporary Judaism. The Jewish material is important, therefore, not just because it allows us to place Jesus in his own time, but because it allows us to interpret his sayings aright. If, then,

The evangelist Mark. Manuscript from Trier, c. 800.

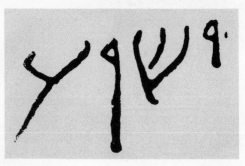

This is how Jesus wrote his name in Hebrew.

we can be sure that there is a Hebrew phrase behind the Greek text of the gospels, we translate that, and not the literal Greek.

This book does not set out to build a bridge between the Jesus of history, and the Christian faith. With no ax to grind, but at the same time without pretending to submerge the author's own personality and milieu—for how can one do that when writing a biography—this book seeks merely to present Jesus here and now to the reader. The present age seems specially well disposed to understand him and his interests. A new sensitivity has been awakened in us by profound fear of the future, and of the present. Today we are receptive to Jesus' reappraisal of all our usual values, and many of us have become aware of the questioning of the moral norm, which is his starting point too. Like Jesus, we feel drawn to the social pariahs, to the sinners. When he says that we must not resist evil because, even by our denial, we only encourage the intrinsically indifferent play of forces within society and the world at large, we men of today at least can understand. If we free ourselves from the chains of dead prejudice, we are able to appreciate his demand for undivided love, not as philanthropic weakness, but as a true psychological consequence.

The enormity of his life, too, speaks to us today: the call of his baptism, the severing of ties with his estranged family and his discovery of a new, sublime sonship, the pandemonium of the sick and possessed, and his death on the cross. Therefore, the words which Matthew (28:20) puts into the mouth of the risen Lord take on for us a new, non-ecclesiastical meaning: "Lo, I am with you always, to the close of the age." *He sees this in*

the light of J²'s continuing influence + relevance to our time.

ANCESTRY

Jesus is the common Greek form of the name Joshua. In Jesus' time the name was pronounced "Jeshua"; and so, we often find Jesus of Nazareth named in ancient Jewish literature. That, almost certainly, was the Galilean pronunciation. After the arrest of Jesus, Peter betrayed himself by his peculiarly Galilean pronunciation. In those days, Jesus was one of the most common of Jewish names. The ancient Jewish historian, Flavius Josephus, for example, mentions twenty men with this name. The first is Joshua of the Bible, Moses' successor who conquered the Holy Land. Out of religious awe, the ancient Jews avoided certain important biblical names such as David, Solomon, Moses, and Aaron. In those days, it may be that the name Jeshua—Jesus— had gained popularity as a kind of substitute for Moses.

Jesus' father, and his brothers likewise, bore very popular names. His brothers[1] were called James, Joses, Judah, and Simon (Mk. 6:3)—the names of the biblical patriarch Jacob and his three sons, as common in those days as Jack and Bill today. Joses is short for Joseph—the name of Jesus' father. Today it would be almost impossible for a Jewish child to be named after its own father, were he alive. In ancient times, by contrast, this was a fairly widespread custom. Jesus' mother was called Mary, which corresponds to the Hebrew, Miriam, in those days also a common name. Although we know few women's names from ancient times—none of the names of Jesus' sisters has come down to us—Josephus mentions eight women called Miriam. The first is the sister of Moses, and the others are all named after her.

The marvelous story of Jesus' birth is to be found in the two literary, independent, versions of Matthew and Luke. It is not to be found in Mark and John, and is not presupposed in any other part of the New Testament. Apart from the New Testament writers, the first to mention the virgin birth is Ignatius of Antioch (d. 107).

13

"Messiah" was linked to θ line of David in Jewish belief

circumstantial dig at M's virginity

As is well known, Jesus Christ means "Jesus the Messiah," and according to ancient Jewish belief, the Messiah was to be a descendant of David—the Son of David. Both Matthew (1:2–16) and Luke (3:23–28) provide a genealogical tree leading back to David.[2] According to both of these genealogies, it is Joseph, not Mary, who is descended from King David. The decisive thing is that both of Joseph's genealogies are found in those gospels that tell the story of the virgin birth: Matthew and Luke. It would seem, therefore, that neither of these evangelists sensed any tension between the descent of Jesus from David through Joseph, and the conception of Jesus without the agency of a human father. We must consider also that the two genealogies agree only from Abraham down to David.[3] The internal problems of both lists, and their considerable differences, leave us with the impression that both genealogies were constructed *ad hoc,* so to speak, in order to prove descent from David.

We know of no one at that time except Jesus[4] whose family was said to be Davidic. It was quite natural that any expected Messiah would retrospectively be legitimized by his followers as the Son of David. This happened to the Messianic pretender, Bar Kochba (d. 135), and it seems to have happened to Jesus also. Even were it possible that the family of Jesus possessed a tradition that they were of David's line, this could hardly have conditioned Jesus' self-consciousness. Jesus of Nazareth as a prince in disguise is a complete absurdity.

Matthew and Luke provide the Davidic genealogy of Jesus; it is they who set the place of his birth in the city of David's birth, Bethlehem. Nevertheless, here the two accounts display important differences. According to Luke (2:4) Jesus' family only traveled to Bethlehem on account of the census. Before the birth of Jesus, they lived in Nazareth to which they returned. According to Matthew, however, the family resided in Bethlehem in Judea before the birth of Jesus, settling in Nazareth only on their return from Egypt (2:23).[5] It would seem, then, that both the tradition that Jesus was born in Bethlehem, and the proof of his Davidic ancestry, arose because many believed that the

14

Partial view of the Church of the Nativity in Bethlehem.

Messiah would be of David's line, and that like David, the Messiah would be born in Bethlehem. This follows plainly from John 7:41–42. This passage tells of some who deny that Jesus is the Messiah, saying: "Is the Christ to come from Galilee? Has not the scripture said that the Christ is descended from David, and comes from Bethlehem, the village where David was?" John, therefore, knew neither that Jesus had been born in Bethlehem nor that he was descended from David. At the same time, this incident shows how people demanded the fulfillment of these two conditions as legitimization of the Messianic claim.

HOW? Isn't the author prejudging their substantiating ū for his evidence?

Or those to whom these words were attributed.

15

Inside the Church of the Nativity, which was erected on the place where, according to tradition, Jesus was born.

Jesus, then, was a Galilean Jew, probably born in Nazareth. Certainly that was where he lived for about thirty years until the time of his baptism by John (Lk. 3:23). He was born either in 27/28 A.D. or 28/29 A.D.[6] It is more difficult to determine the duration of his public ministry, the period between his baptism and crucifixion. On the evidence of the first three gospels, it appears that this period extended to not more than one year. Following John, on the other hand, we would have to assume that it ran to two, or even three years. It has become fairly clear today that John the theologian had little intention of being a historian, and so it would be unwise to accept his chronology or

16

his geographical framework without examination.[7] In any case we have to ask also whether the first three gospels do intend to provide a historical and geographical scheme, and to what extent such a scheme is conditioned by the theological presuppositions of the individual evangelists.[8] There is material evidence to suggest that on these points the synoptists are to be trusted. Jesus may have worked in Judea and in Jerusalem before his final journey to death, but his real sphere of operation was in Galilee on the northwest shore of Lake Gennesaret. It will also become evident that the events are best understood on the presumption that the baptism and the crucifixion were separated by only a short space of time. There are scholars who assume that Jesus died at Easter in the year 30 or 33. Most probably, then, Jesus was baptized in 28/29, and died in the year 30.

As we have seen, Jesus had four brothers and some sisters. The family at Nazareth, therefore, included at least seven children.' If one accepts the virgin birth as historical, and also concedes that the brethren of Jesus were his true brothers and sisters, the conclusion must be accepted that Jesus was Mary's first-born child. Even those who regard the nativity narratives of Matthew and Luke as unhistorical, must consider that Jesus may well have been the eldest of the family. Luke (2:22–24) reports that the parents of Jesus took him to Jerusalem shortly after his birth to present him to the Lord, as the law prescribed: "Every male that opens the womb shall be called holy to the Lord." It is true that one could redeem one's first-born through an offering to a priest anywhere,[9] but there were devout people who took this opportunity of making a pilgrimage with their son to the temple in Jerusalem. Did Luke or his source invent this story to proclaim the virgin birth, or was Jesus, in fact, Mary's eldest child?

which he does in rejecting the ref to Bethlehem

It is almost certain that Jesus' father died before Jesus was baptized. He may have died when Jesus was still quite a child. When Jesus' public ministry began, we meet his mother and his brethren, but there is no mention of his father. According to Luke (2:41–51), Joseph was still alive when Jesus was twelve

17

years old. "Now his parents went to Jerusalem every year at the feast of the Passover. And when he was twelve years old, they went up according to the custom; and when the feast was ended, as they were returning, the boy Jesus stayed behind in Jerusalem. His parents did not know it, but supposing him to be in the company they went a day's journey, and they sought him among their kinsfolk and acquaintances; and when they did not find him, they returned to Jerusalem, seeking him. After three days they found him in the temple, sitting among the teachers, listening to them and asking them questions; and all who heard him were amazed at his understanding and his answers."

This anecdote from the life of the boy, Jesus, has special significance: it is a story of the precocious scholar, one might almost say, of a young talmudist. Today a Jewish boy is regarded as an adult when he turns thirteen; but in those days a boy of twelve could be regarded as grown up. Luke's story may well be true. I myself have heard the widow of a great rabbinic scholar, A. Aptowitzer, tell how her husband was lost when his parents were visiting an annual fair. In the early hours of the morning, they found him in a school keenly disputing scholarly problems with the rabbis. This woman had certainly never read St. Luke. If I am not mistaken, the Indian philosopher Gupta tells a similar story in his autobiography.

The anecdote Luke tells of the boy, Jesus, does not contradict the rest of what we know about Jesus' Jewish education. It will be affirmed with some justification that Jesus' disciples were "uneducated, common men" (Acts 4:13). This led to the assertion—made, indeed, by the historically less reliable John (7:15)—that Jesus himself was uneducated, that he had "never studied." Viewing Jesus' sayings against the background of contemporary Jewish learning, however, it is easy to observe that Jesus was far from uneducated. He was perfectly at home both in holy scripture, and in oral tradition, and knew how to apply this scholarly heritage. Jesus' Jewish education was incomparably superior to that of St. Paul.

External corroboration of Jesus' Jewish scholarship is pro-

The evangelist Luke. Manuscript from Würzburg, c. 800.

called Rabbi vided by the fact that, although he was not an approved scribe,[10] men were accustomed to address him as "Rabbi," "my teacher."[11] "The form of address 'Rabbi' was in common use in those days, and was specially in favor to describe scholars and teachers of the Torah. It had not yet become restricted to expert and ordained teachers."[12] The generation following Jesus was the first to know the title as an academic degree. Jesus did not approve of the pleasure so many Pharisees took in being addressed as rabbi. "And," he said, "call no man your father on earth, for you have one Father, who is in heaven" (Mt. 23:6–12). In those days "Abba" was another common form of address. In the generation before Jesus, a scribe had said much the same thing: "Love manual work and hate rabbinism."[13] Many shared this view. Arrogance may often have been found among the scribes, but they were not effete academicians. They demanded that everyone teach his son a trade, and many of them were themselves artisans. Joiners were regarded as particularly learned. If a difficult problem was under discussion, they would ask: "Is there a joiner among us, or the son of a joiner, who can solve the problem for us?"[14] Jesus was either a joiner or the son of a joiner; most likely he was both. This in itself is no proof that either he or his father was learned, but it counts against the common sweetly idyllic notion of Jesus as a naïve and amiable, simple manual workman.

Maintains Jesus rejected his family Nietzsche was right when he wrote: "All the attempts I know of to construct the history of a 'soul' from the Gospels seem to me to imply a deplorable levity in psychological matters."[15] There is, however, a psychological element in the life of Jesus that we may not ignore: his rejection of the family into which he was born. This element is to be found even in the historically less reliable John. At the marriage feast in Cana, Jesus' mother asked him to produce wine, and he replied: "O woman, what have you to do with me?" (2:4).[16] In a freshly discovered apocryphal narrative, this theme of tension between Jesus and his family is heightened almost intolerably. This[17] tells that, as Jesus was being crucified, his mother Mary and her sons James, Simon,

Nazareth.

and Judah, came and stood before him. Hanging upon the cross, he said to her: "Take your sons and go away!" The synoptists, too, tell us something about this tension. On one occasion, his mother and his brethren came and asked to speak to him. He turned to the disciples and said: "Here are my mother and my brethren! For whoever does the will of my Father in heaven is my brother, and sister, and mother" (Mt. 12:46–50; cf. Lk. 11:27–28). Jesus applied this experience to others as well: "Truly, I say to you, there is no man who has left house or wife or brothers or parents or children, for the sake of the kingdom of God, who will not receive manifold more in this time, and in the age to come eternal life" (Lk. 18:28–30). There is another saying on the same subject that does not sound so inhuman in Hebrew as in translation: "If any one comes to me and does not hate his own father and mother and wife and children and brothers and sisters . . . he cannot be my disciple" (Lk. 14:26). Jesus knew that uncompromising religious commitment was bound to break family ties, all the more as he was certain that the end was in sight. To another he said, "Follow me." But he said, "Lord, let me first go and bury my father." But he said to him, "Leave the dead to bury their own dead . . ." Another said, "I will follow you Lord; but first let me say farewell to those at my home." Jesus said to him, "No one who puts his hand to the plough and looks back is fit for the kingdom of God" (Lk. 9:59–62).

As we have seen, an emotion-laden tension seems to have arisen between Jesus and his family, and it would appear to have been this psychological fact—the background to which we do not know—that powerfully contributed to his personal decision that was so decisive for mankind. Mark reduces this psychological background to a very simple formula: when Jesus left his workshop and set off to preach the kingdom of God, his family thought he had gone mad. Mark reports that his friends "went out to seize him, for they said, 'He is beside himself'" (Mk. 3:21). This passage is unreliable, however, for it is a rather abstruse contribution of the evangelist.[18] The real core of all this is probably the fact that his family regarded the mission which led the Son to death as a dangerous illusion (Jn. 7:5). Jesus correctly suspected that his own kith and kin would not believe in him. For this reason, he did not return home after his baptism, but went to Capernaum. When he left that town to visit his native town, he only proved that no one is a prophet in his own country; for when he taught in the synagogue at Nazareth, the people asked where the son of Joseph had obtained all of his wisdom; and he was unable to perform any miracles there on account of their unbelief. If psychology is right, this is all quite intelligible.

What happened to Jesus' family after his death? A doubtful

22

Christ being mocked by the Gentiles. The Crucified has an ass' head
because of the calumny that the Jews worshiped an ass. Graffito from
the first half of the third century.

אוֹמְרַיָא / דָיָא מְנָא עֲשָׂאת דָיָא עֲרְעָא אַוָּא עֲווּד צָוְּוד דָיָא שָׂאוּד מְּדְּ יְזָוּוד צָלָמֵי וְבָוּ
קָל קוֹלָא בַּעֲבָר נַע אֵיךְ אֲחֹוֹד וְאָשׂוֹד בָּעֲרְבוּת
גְמְלָא לְאֵוֹאֵינוּ צוֹל אַא מֵעֲשָׂא וְצוֹי אַד וְגַבְשֵׂין אֲשָׂלוּ וְזָאֵוֹ אֵיעֲזָבְבָעֲשָׂוּ
וְאֵיחָיַ מְמַד לְבַקְעָא וְגַלָ... זְוֹוּד אֵתָאַד וֹאָאֵן צָל בְּשָׂד מָאֲזָע נָא פָּא
אֲזֵיאַ וְבַד
קוֹל אֵמֶר דָּא זְאֵמְרוּ נַע אַתָא אַו זְאֵלָאֵבְעֵד זְעֵזְ זָל אָמוֹזְמְעֵזְזְעֵין

"A voice cries . . ." (Isaiah 40:3). From a Dead Sea scroll.

Haenchen does NOT say its doubtful

report (Acts 1:14)[19] tells us that Mary, the mother of Jesus, and his brethren joined the apostles in Jerusalem. The Lord's brother, James, came to believe as a result of a resurrection appearance.[20] In 62 A.D. James died for faith in his brother. He was murdered by a Sadducean high priest.[21] The other brothers were later converted to faith, and with their wives, they accepted the hospitality of the congregations (1 Cor. 9:5). Having recognized their dead brother as the Messiah, the brothers of the Lord then realized that they too were of David's line. An old account[22] tells us that the Emperor Domitian regarded the grandsons of the Lord's brother, Judah, with suspicion because they belonged to the Jewish royal house. The Emperor is supposed to have interrogated them in Rome, but set them free when he discovered that they were only poor peasants. They were leaders of Christian churches apparently in Galilee, and they lived until the reign of Trajan. James, the brother of the Lord, was succeeded as head of the Church in Jerusalem by Simeon, a cousin of Jesus. After Jesus' death, his family had, therefore, overcome their disbelief, and took an honorable place in the young Jewish-Christian community. We can understand their action: it might be dangerous, indeed, to live as the Redeemer's relative within an ordered society; but it was simpler to do so than to see a brother or a son as different from oneself. Despite all her inability to understand her son, Jesus' mother behaved very properly. The dreaded catastrophe came, and her own heart was pierced by a sword.[23] Did she find complete consolation later through faith in her risen son, and in the hope that she would see him again?

regarding "Brothers" cf pg 13.

24

THE BAPTISM

In those days, John the Baptist[24] went out into the wilderness preaching a baptism of repentance for forgiveness of sins. The prophecy of Isaiah (40:3) was being fulfilled: "The voice of one crying in the wilderness: Prepare the way of the Lord" (see Mk. 1:2–4). For the Essenes, too, whose writings have been discovered near the Dead Sea, this prophecy was a call "to depart from the habitations of men of sin, to go into the wilderness to prepare the way of the Lord."[25] John was so close to the Essenes that it is possible that at one time he may have belonged to one of their communities which he left later because he disapproved of the sectarian separatism of the Essenes, and wanted to offer the opportunity of repentance and forgiveness of sins to the whole of Israel. Thus crowds streamed out from far and near to the grim austere prophet of the wilderness; they listened to his threatening penitential sermons, confessed their sins, and were baptized by him in the river Jordan. His powerful influence over the people led him to his execution by Herod Antipas, son of King Herod the Great. Josephus reports:[26] "Herod, who feared lest the great influence John had over the people might put it into his power and inclination to raise a rebellion (for they seemed ready to do anything he should advise), thought it best, by putting him to death, to prevent any mischief he might cause, and not bring himself into difficulties by sparing a man who might make him repent of it when it should be too late." We learn more about the death of John from the gospels.[27]

The thing that most attracted men to John the Baptist was the baptism he conferred. Many hoped that the immersion would expiate their sins, and thus, they would escape the coming wrath of God's judgment. However, John first demanded true penitence. According to Josephus, John was a holy man "who called upon the Jews to purify themselves in baptism, to dedicate themselves to virtue, to the practice of justice towards each other and

25

QVOD VATES BELLVM CREVIT NOH ESSE DVELLVM
CODIDIT & MVLTIS VOBIS QVI CERHERE VVLTIS
EST IOSEPHVS DICTVS FERT LIBRVM CORPORE PICTVS

The Jewish historian Flavius Josephus. Manuscript from Toulouse.

piety towards God, so that the washing would be acceptable to
him, if they made use of it, not for the putting away of
some sins, but for the purification of the body: supposing still
that the soul was thoroughly purified beforehand by righteousness." This is exactly in line with the Essene view: their baptismal baths—as elsewhere in Israel—merely washed ritual

26

Baptismal cistern in the Essene settlement at Qumran.

uncleanness from the body; but in the Essene view, a sin committed brings ritual uncleanness, and so, "no one may enter the water . . . unless he has repented of his evil, because uncleanness attaches to all transgressions against His Word."[28] Only he "who bows his soul to the law of God, has his flesh purified by the sprinkling of the purifying waters, and is sanctified in the water

John baptizing Jesus. From a Roman catacomb, early second century.

of purity."[29] Or again—almost in the very words that express the view of John the Baptist: water can cleanse the body only if the soul has first been purified through righteousness. But what is it in repentance that purifies the soul? "By the spirit of holiness . . . a man is cleansed from all sins."[30] In this way, Essene baptism linked repentance with the forgiveness of sins, and the latter with the Holy Spirit. As John's notion of baptism coincided with that of the Essenes, like them he too saw the Holy Spirit at work in baptism.[31]

We can well imagine the holy excitement of that crowd who had listened to the very words of the Baptist. Having confessed their sins, they plunged their defiled bodies in the cleansing water of the river, awaiting the gift of the Holy Spirit who would now cleanse their souls from all the filth of sin. Could it be that none of them would have a special pneumatic-ecstatic experience in that hour when the Spirit of God touched them? "Now when all the people were baptized, and when Jesus also had been baptized and was praying, the heaven was opened, and the Holy Spirit descended upon him in bodily form, as a dove, and a voice came[32] from heaven, 'Thou art my beloved Son[33]; with thee I am well pleased'." Thus spoke the heavenly voice according to Matthew (3:17) and Mark (1:11). And yet many scholars[34] are right in thinking that in the original account, the heavenly voice announced to Jesus: "Behold my servant, whom I uphold, my chosen, in whom my soul delights; I have put my Spirit upon him, he will bring forth justice to the nations" (Isaiah 42:1). This form is probably the original for the reason also that the prophetic word fits the situation. Echoing voices were not an uncommon phenomenon among the Jews of those days, and frequently these voices were heard to utter verses from scripture. Endowment with the Holy Spirit, accompanied by an ecstatic experience, was apparently no unique experience among those who were baptized in John's presence in the Jordan. If Jews really did hear these words from Isaiah, the phrase "I have put my Spirit upon him" was a wonderful confirmation of the gift of the Holy Spirit. There was something else, however, that possesses unique significance. If we accept the traditional form of the heavenly message, Jesus is described as "My Son"; but if the heavenly voice intoned the words of Isaiah, Jesus must have understood that he was being set apart as the Servant of God, the Chosen One. For him the gift of the Holy Spirit, which was part of John's baptism, held another special significance that was to become decisive for his future life. Neither Son nor Servant nor Chosen One were exclusively Messianic titles—the last two could also denote the dignity of the prophetic office—, but by these titles, Jesus learned that he was now chosen, called, set apart. Nothing that we have learned casts any doubt upon the historicity of Jesus' experience at his baptism in the Jordan.

According to Mark (1:9) and Matthew (3.13), Jesus came

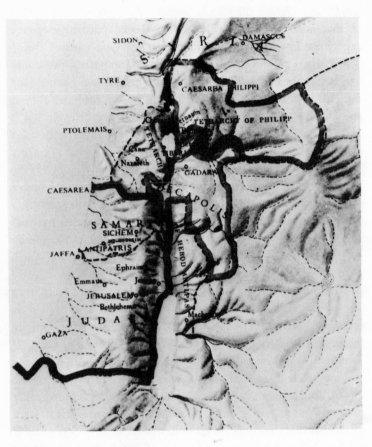

Palestine in the time of Jesus.

to John from his home in Nazareth; and, if we are to believe the words of the archangel reported by Luke (1:36), Mary was related to John's mother. We cannot learn any more than this about the psychological background to Jesus' decision to join the crowd and be baptized by John. On the other hand, if we use the documents properly, we can form a fairly clear idea of what happened to Jesus after his baptism and call. The only serious problem seems to be that we have no reliable report of the place of the Baptist's activities,[35] and, moreover, it is very likely that

The wilderness of Judea between Jerusalem and Jericho.

this prophet of the wilderness moved about quite a lot. The simplest thing seems to be to assume that Jesus was baptized by John not far from the point where the Jordan enters the Lake of Gennesaret in the north. There too, at Bethsaida, was the home of the brothers Andrew and Peter, whom, according to John (1:40–44), Jesus met at his baptism. Peter, and his brother Andrew, and the brothers James and John, the sons of Zebedee, also fishermen on the Lake of Gennesaret, then became his first disciples. Peter was married to a woman from nearby

Capernaum where he lived in her mother's house.[36] This woman, too, became a believer, after Jesus cured her of a fever, and her house became almost a second home for Jesus. Later, after his unsuccessful visit to his native Nazareth, Jesus returned to the district around Capernaum.

The geographical setting for Jesus' public ministry becomes apparent perhaps from the place of his baptism, and probably from his acquaintance with Peter. This is not a theological, but a strictly factual background. It is confirmed by Jesus' own words from the so-called *Sayings of Jesus*. "Then he began to upbraid the cities where most of his mighty works had been done, because they did not repent. 'Woe to you, Chorazin! woe to you, Bethsaida! for if the mighty works done in you had been done in Tyre and Sidon, they would have repented long ago in sackcloth and ashes. But I tell you, it shall be more tolerable on the day of judgment for Tyre and Sidon than for you. And you, Capernaum, will you be exalted to heaven? You shall be brought down to Hades. For if the mighty works done in you had been done in Sodom, it would have remained to this day. But I tell you that it shall be more tolerable on the day of judgment for the land of Sodom than for you'" (Mt. 11:20–24; Lk. 10:12–15). Nearby Chorazin is not mentioned anywhere else in the New Testament, and the wretched Mary Magdalene "from whom seven demons had gone out" (Lk. 8:2), came from the neighboring Magdala. The northwest corner of the Sea of Galilee was densely populated and well cultivated—the wheat of Chorazin was famous. Many fishermen lived there, and sailed across to the east bank where they caught a rich harvest of fish. The inhabitants of this district were no rude backwoodsmen.

More important than settling the geographical setting of Jesus' public ministry is defining the mutual relation between John the Baptist and Jesus after the baptism. Only when we have cleared up some common errors can we portray Jesus in his true significance. The root of the distortion lies in the chronology of salvation history[37] found in Mark. Because, in the Christian view, John the Baptist was justifiably regarded as the

Ruins of the synagogue at Chorazin.

precursor of Jesus, and because Jesus' entry on the scene did follow that of John, Mark makes John the precursor of Jesus in the literal sense. Thus, according to Mark, Jesus could appear publicly only after John had been arrested. "Now after John was arrested, Jesus came into Galilee, preaching the gospel of God" (Mk. 1:14). Matthew goes a step further. Since according to Mark, whom he believed (see Mt. 4:12–13), John had been arrested before the first appearance of Jesus, John was able to ask if Jesus was the one who was to come, only after he was already in prison. On this point, therefore, Matthew "improves upon" the *Sayings* (Mt. 11:2; cf. Lk. 7:18), and because Matthew displays a general tendency to assimilate the words of John and the sayings of Jesus to each other,[38] he puts Jesus' preaching, word for word, in the Baptist's mouth (Mt. 3:2; cf.

4:17). The picture having thus been displaced gradually, scholars then try to interpret the distortion that has arisen, historically and psychologically. Mark's false chronology is usually taken to prove that Jesus' prime purpose in stepping into public life was to fill the gap left in Israel by the arrest of the Baptist. This impression then seems to find confirmation in Matthew, for at first, according to this gospel, Jesus merely continued to preach John's message. If that were so, it was the height of human tragedy when, shortly before his death, John, who had spent his whole life waiting for the Messiah, received news of Jesus' emergence, and sent messengers to him. No wonder that Flaubert described this moving scene in his story, *Herodias*!

In this way, the original historical picture is altered first of all for theological reasons by Mark and Matthew, then through the psychological reinterpretation of many scholars. The less reliable John, in fact, knows that "John had not yet been put in prison" (3:24). Luke and his sources, too, never report that Jesus appeared only after John had disappeared. Having, then, removed the secondary distortions, we can proceed to tell the story of the beginning of Jesus' public ministry.

John the Baptist certainly had a circle of disciples; but obviously most of the men whom he baptized in the Jordan left him after their baptism and went home. John did not want to found a sect, but thought it better to send each man back to his own trade (Lk. 3:10–14). On the other hand, Jesus did not return to his former life after the voice at his baptism had announced his election, but "From that time Jesus began to preach, saying, 'Repent, for the kingdom of God is at hand'" (Mt. 4:17). He called his disciples, taught in the synagogues, "and they brought him all the sick . . . and he healed them" (Mt. 4:17–25).[39]

It is possible that John the Baptist believed himself to be the prophet who was to come at the end of time. The people saw him as the biblical prophet Elijah who was to precede the Messiah. He himself preached that one would soon come who was stronger than he, and who would inaugurate the judgment.

The synagogue of Capernaum, partly restored.

When John heard of the excitement over Jesus in the villages around the Sea of Galilee—so the sources tell us[40]—he sent two of his disciples to Jesus to ask: "Are you he who is to come, or shall we look for another?" In those days, it was a Jewish custom to send not one but two men on a commission. Jesus, too, sent his disciples out by twos (Mk. 6:7; Lk. 10:1), and this custom was continued by Christians on their early missionary journeys.[41] On the other hand, the text of the Baptist's question about Jesus can hardly be the original. To speak of the Messiah as "he who is to come" without further specifications is possible in Greek, it is true, but hardly in Hebrew or Aramaic. Yet the original meaning of the question seems to be more or less preserved in the present form. At all events John wanted to know: did the appearance of Jesus herald the end of time, or was there still someone else to come? The old account[42] tells us that Jesus sent this reply to the Baptist: "Go and tell John what you have seen and heard: the blind receive their sight, the lame walk, lepers are cleansed, and the deaf hear, the dead are raised up, the poor have good news preached to them. And blessed is he who takes no offense at me."

What is important is that Jesus affirmed in principle the Baptist's question about the eschatological meaning of his activities, but without explicitly declaring that he was the coming Messiah. He established his claim to the eschatological office by pointing to his preaching of salvation and to his supernatural works of healing. Jesus saw these things as an unmistakable sign that the era of salvation had already dawned. "But if it is by the finger of God that I cast out demons, then the kingdom of God has come upon you" (Lk. 11:20). Disease is of the devil; and the kingdom of God comes when Satan is conquered and rendered powerless. According to Luke (10:18), Jesus once said: "I saw Satan fall like lightning from heaven." According to a book[43] written when Jesus was a child: "Then will his kingdom over all creation appear, Satan will be destroyed and grief will depart with him." The coming of the kingdom is thus bound up with the overthrow of Satan and his spirits; when Jesus heals the sick and casts out unclean spirits he is the victorious conqueror who makes real the kingdom of God.[44] "When a strong man, fully armed, guards his own palace, his goods are in peace; but when one stronger than he assaults him and overcomes him, he takes away his armor in which he trusted, and divides his spoil. He who is not with me is against me, and he who does not gather with me scatters" (Lk. 11:21–23).

In addition to miracles of healing, Jesus gives the Baptist a second proof of his claim: the poor have salvation preached to them. This is an allusion to words of the prophet Isaiah (61:1–2) which were specially important to Jesus: "The Spirit of the Lord God is upon me, because the Lord has anointed me to bring good tidings to the afflicted; he has sent me to bind up the brokenhearted, to proclaim liberty to the captives, and the

Manuscript scroll with the words from the prophet Isaiah (61:1–2), which Jesus applied to himself. From the discoveries at Qumran.

opening of the prison to those who are bound; to proclaim the year of the Lord's favor, and the day of vengeance of our God; to comfort all who mourn." These were the words that Jesus read in the synagogue at the very start of his ministry. Then he rolled up the scroll, and handed it back to the attendant, sat down and said, "Today this scripture has been fulfilled in your hearing" (Lk. 4:16–21). These words of the prophet ring out, too, in Jesus' beatitudes, in which he opens the kingdom of heaven to the poor in spirit, and the meek, and gives comfort to them that mourn. It was to them that the good news of Jesus was sent; so it was called in Greek *evangelion*, because this substantive derives from the verb used in the verse from Isaiah to denote the preaching of salvation. For Jesus, this passage from scripture was the bridge between his calling, as he was baptized by John in the Jordan, and his present designation: he knew that the Spirit of the Lord had come upon him, because the Lord had anointed him to proclaim salvation to the meek and the poor.

As John's messengers were departing to report Jesus' answer, "Jesus began to speak to the crowds concerning John: 'What did you go out into the wilderness to behold? A reed shaken by the wind? Why then did you go out? To see a man clothed in soft raiment? Behold, those who wear soft raiment are in kings' houses. Why then did you go out? To see a prophet? Yes, I tell you, and more than a prophet. This is he of whom it is written,[45] "Behold, I send my messenger before thy face, who shall prepare thy way before thee." Truly I say to you, among those born of women there has risen no one greater than John the Baptist; yet he who is least in the kingdom of heaven is greater than he. From the days of John the Baptist until now the kingdom of heaven has suffered violence, and men of violence take it by force. For all the prophets and the law prophesied until John; and if you are willing to accept it, he is Elijah who is to come. He who has ears to hear, let him hear' " (Mt. 11:7–15).

Buber once said, in a conversation, that if a man has the gift of listening, he can hear the voice of Jesus himself speaking in the late accounts of the gospels. This authentic note can, I think, be detected in Jesus' comments on the Baptist. These are at once simple and profound, naïve and full of paradox, tempestuous and yet calm. Can anyone plumb their ultimate depths?

Jesus was addressing those who had made their pilgrimage out into the wilderness to see the new prophet. That was no place

The first of the caves in which Essene manuscripts were discovered.

to find courtiers dressed in fine clothes, who live in palaces, and bend like a reed in the wind to every change of opinion. We observe that the imagery is taken from a well-known fable of Aesop, with which the rabbis, too, were familiar.[46] The reed outlives the storm because it bends to the wind, whereas a stronger tree, that refuses to bend, is often uprooted by the storm. Now we know who was the target for Jesus' scorn: Herod Antipas and his fawning courtiers, against whom the unbending fearless desert prophet, dressed in a garment of camel hair, hurled his preaching of doom. It can surely be an accident that Jesus recast a fable of Aesop: clearly he regarded the tetrarch and his court as a kind of "animal farm." Later, in Aesop's style, he was to describe Herod as "that fox" (Lk. 13:32).

In Jesus' view, John was a prophet, if you like, the one who was preparing the way of God at the end of time, the Elijah who was to return. With John the end-time begins—the decisive eruption into the history of the world. All the prophets have prophesied until the time of John the Baptist; but from now on, "the kingdom of heaven has suffered violence, and men of violence take it by force." These enigmatic words are connected with the saying of the prophet Micah (2:13): "He who opens the breach will go up before them; they will break through and pass the gate, going out by it. Their king will pass on before them, the Lord at their head." A medieval commentator, David Kimchi, put the following interpretation upon this verse: "The 'one who opens up the breach' is Elijah and 'their king' is the scion of David." According to this interpretation, which Jesus seems to have known, Elijah was to come first to open the breach, and he would be followed by those who broke through with their king, the Messiah. According to Jesus, the Elijah-John has already come, and those men who have the courage of decision now take the kingdom by force. We will have more to say about this saying of Jesus.

With John's coming, the kingdom of heaven broke through, and yet, although John was the greatest among the children of men, the least in the kingdom of heaven is greater than he. John the Baptist made the breach through which the kingdom of God could break, but he himself was never a member of that kingdom. We might put it thus: John was still a member of the older generation, not of the messianic kingdom. This paradoxical insight, part of Jesus' illumination by the heavenly voice at his baptism, linked him at once, no doubt, with the Baptist, and invested him with a new and separate function. Jesus could not become a disciple of John, but would have to move off to the villages around the Sea of Galilee, and preach the kingdom of heaven himself.

Now we understand why Jesus' reply to the Baptist's enquiry ended with a warning: "Blessed is he who takes no offense at me." The Hebrew verb, in those days expanded to mean "to be led into sin, to go astray from the right understanding of the will of God," is rendered literally by "to stumble." Following a later document (1 Pet. 2:7–8), Jesus is, as it were, the touchstone, a cornerstone for believers, a rock of offense, and a stone of stumbling (cf. Lk. 20:18) for unbelievers. When the Baptist sent his enquiry to Jesus, Jesus rightly guessed that John the Baptist could not go along with him, for he, the greatest member of the former generation, did not belong to the kingdom of God. It may even be that Jesus had concrete indications of this fact. We are not told what the Baptist's reaction was to Jesus' message, and the movement he started carried on an independent life parallel to that of emergent Christianity.

As we have seen, many thought that John was Elijah come again. The Old Testament itself tells us that Elijah never died, but was transported up to heaven. How, then, could this immortal one, having returned at the end of time as John, be irrevocably killed by Herod? There were indeed men who thought that John the Baptist had risen from the dead (Mk. 6:14) and had reappeared in Jesus. It is obvious that many of John's disciples shared this belief in their master's resurrection. John's own preaching rules out the possibility that he regarded himself as the Messiah; he looked for another to come who was greater than himself (Lk. 3:16). Yet, there were those among

41

his disciples who, even during his life, toyed with the idea that he was the greater. At all events, after his death there was evidence of belief in the Baptist as the Messiah. Clearly, however, because he belonged to a priestly line, he was not regarded as the Davidic, but as the priestly Messiah.

The logic of the accounts requires that Herod must have been quick to see the danger that the Baptist represented; thus he did not leave him free long. Jesus' activity, too, after John's arrest, was obviously restricted to a very short space of time. Herod, the fox, had not been asleep. After he had executed John, "Herod the tetrarch heard about the fame of Jesus; and he said to his servants, 'This is John the Baptist, he has been raised from the dead' " (Mt. 14:1). Later, some of the Pharisees warned Jesus that Herod was seeking his life. Thereupon, Jesus sent word to Herod that he would spend two or three days more in the district, and then move on to Jerusalem, "for it cannot be that a prophet should perish away from Jerusalem" (Lk. 13:31). As we shall see, Herod had his share in the blame for the crucifixion.

After John's execution, Jesus pointed out to his disciples the tragic connection between John's execution, and the end which threatened himself. Unfortunately we do not possess the original text of this saying. "And the disciples asked him, 'Then why do the scribes say that first Elijah must come?' He replied, 'Elijah does come, and he is to restore all things; but I tell you that Elijah has already come, and they did not know him, but did to him whatever they pleased. So also the Son of man will suffer at their hands.' Then the disciples understood that he was speaking to them of John the Baptist" (Mt. 17:10–13).

Earlier than this, at the beginning of his ministry, when John the Baptist was still preaching in the wilderness, Jesus had compared himself with John the Baptist: "But to what shall I compare this generation? It is like children sitting in the market places calling to their playmates, 'We piped to you, and you did not dance; we wailed, and you did not mourn.'[47] For John came neither eating nor drinking, and they say, 'He has a demon'; the Son of man came eating and drinking, and they say, 'Behold, a

glutton and a drunkard, a friend of tax collectors and sinners!'
Yet wisdom is justified by her deeds" (Mt. 11:16–19). It was
impossible to please anybody; they said that the ascetic desert
preacher, John, was mad—as they said later that Jesus was
possessed by the spirit of evil—and they found fault with Jesus,
too, on account of his openness to the world. From this saying
of Jesus we learn indirectly that the content of each man's
preaching was closely linked with his character: the good news
of love was related to Jesus' Socratic nature; penitential preaching was related to John's sombre inclination to asceticism.

THE LAW

Paul and his entourage "went through the region of Phrygia and Galatia, having been forbidden by the Holy Spirit to speak the word in Asia . . . ; so, passing by Mysia, they went down to Troas. And a vision appeared to Paul in the night: a man of Macedonia was standing beseeching him and saying, 'Come over to Macedonia and help us'" (Acts 16:6–10).

This episode in Paul's mission to the heathen was of enormous importance: it was the will of God to spread Christianity to Europe. Thus Christianity became at first a Graeco-Roman, and later, a European religion. In contrast to Judaism and the religions of eastern Asia that originated in ancient Persia, Western culture sets no store by ritual or ceremonial prescriptions concerning "food and drink and various ablutions" (Heb. 9:10), for, in the European view, one may "eat whatever is sold in the meat market without raising any question on the ground of conscience. For 'the earth is the Lord's, and everything in it'" (1 Cor. 10:25–26). One of the tasks taken up by Paulinism, and other movements in early Christianity, was the creation of an ideological superstructure upon this concept of freedom from the law. In the course of the history of Christianity, the superstructure has changed, it is true; but on the whole, it has had to remain; for this "liberalism" is a characteristic of European civilization. Had Christianity spread first to the eastern Asiatic regions, it would have had to develop a ritual and ceremonial law based on the Jewish law in order to become a genuine religion in that part of the world. It would be a mistake, therefore, to deny a genuine understanding to the many Christian thinkers and scholars who have felt obliged to deal with the fact that the founder of their religion was a Jew, faithful to the law, and who never had to face the necessity of adapting his Judaism to the European way of life. For Jesus there was, of course, the peculiar problem of his relationship to the law and its

44

Moses. From the synagogue at Dura Europos, c. 243 A.D.

precepts; but this arises for every believing Jew who takes his Judaism seriously. In the gospels, we shall see how Jesus' attitude to the law has often become unrecognizable as the result of a fresh illumination, and later touching up. The synoptic gospels, however, if read through the eyes of their own time, still portray a picture of Jesus as a Jew who was faithful to the law.

Few people seem to realize that in the synoptic gospels, Jesus is never shown in conflict with current practice of the law—with the single exception of the plucking of ears of corn on the sabbath. On this incident, Luke (6:1–5) is the closest to the original account: "On a sabbath, while he was going through the grainfields, his disciples plucked and ate some ears of grain, rubbing them in their hands. But some of the Pharisees said, 'Why are you doing[48] what is not lawful to do on the sabbath?' " The general opinion was that on the sabbath it was permissible to pick up fallen ears of grain, and rub them between the fingers; but according to Rabbi Jehuda, also a Galilean, it was also permissible to rub them in one's hand.[49] Some of the Pharisees, therefore, found fault with Jesus' disciples for behaving in accordance with their Galilean tradition. The Greek translator of the original was unacquainted with the customs of the people, and to make the scene more vivid, added the statement about plucking the corn as well, thus introducing the one and only act of transgression of the law recorded in the synoptic tradition.

In the case of washing hands before a meal, the synoptic tradition is not to blame for the misunderstanding. The precept about washing hands was neither part of written nor of oral teaching. In Jesus' time the precept ran: "Washing hands before a meal is a matter of choice, ablution after a meal is obligatory."[50] This custom concerned rabbinic regulations which are first found, perhaps, in the generation before Jesus. Even the most bigoted village Pharisee of those days would have shaken his head uncomprehendingly had anyone asserted that, because Jesus' disciples did not always wash their hands before eating, Jesus had broken the law of Moses. Viewed from the standpoint of the gradation of Jewish precepts, the scribes in conversation with Jesus, described the washing of hands as no more than "a tradition of the fathers" (Mk. 7:5). Jesus, too, was using the concepts of his own time when he described the rabbinical prescription of washing of hands—not obligatory in those days—as "a tradition of men" (Mk. 7:8) in contrast to the commandments of written and oral teaching.

The prescription of the washing of hands before a meal was not generally binding in those days for the simple reason that it was one of those rules of purification that did not affect all Jews, but only those particular groups of Jews who had accepted them voluntarily for life. The degree and extent of this obligation varied. Under strict obligation were the Pharisees, a society whose rules of ritual purity were still much looser than those of the Essene community. Thus, it was natural that in the debate on washing of hands, Jesus should have had in mind this very category of purification: "not what goes into the mouth defiles a man, but what comes out of the mouth, this defiles a man" (Mt. 15:11). What Jesus said has, therefore, nothing to do with a supposed abrogation of the Judaic law, but is part of a criticism of the Pharisees. The general truth that strict observation of ritual purity can itself encourage moral laxity, was applicable even in Jesus' day. A Jewish writer[51] of those days certainly had the Pharisees in mind when he spoke of "pernicious and criminal men, who claim to be righteous . . . pleasing themselves, hypocritical in all their ways . . . their hands and hearts are all corrupt, and their mouths are full of boasting—and yet they complain: do not touch me lest you make me unclean." Here, as with Jesus, the contrast between morally unclean thought and speech, and the craving for ritual purity is stressed. Jesus spoke on this topic on another occasion: "Woe to you, scribes and Pharisees, hypocrites! for you cleanse the outside of the cup and of the plate, but inside they are full of extortion and rapacity. You blind Pharisee! first cleanse the inside of the cup and of the plate, that the outside also may be clean" (Mt. 23:25–26). And he called them "blind guides, straining at a gnat and swallowing a camel!" (Mt. 23:24). This last saying sounds like a proverb. Perhaps Jesus' saying about interior and external purity was not original either.

If we are right in thinking that this saying is an important one, we ought to enquire into the precise meaning it had for Jesus himself. Following the custom, Jesus used to pronounce a blessing over wine and bread. Did he, at the same time, believe that material things are in themselves religiously indifferent? A few decades later Rabban Jochanan ben Sakkai said to his pupils: "In life it is not the dead who make you unclean, nor is it water, but the ordinance of the king of kings that purifies; God has said: I have established my statute, I have settled my ordinance; no man has the right to transgress my ordinance; for it is written[52]: "This is the statute of the law which the Lord has commanded."[53] Jesus would not have spoken thus—for one thing, it is too rationalistic. We may say—provisionally—that for Jesus, moral values far overshadowed all ritual values; but that is far from the whole truth. Would Jesus, in any case, think in such sharply defined theoretical categories?

On the matter of washing hands[54] and plucking ears of corn, it was the disciples, not the master, who were less strict in their observance of the law. Even this is not usually noticed. When his disciples' negligence was pointed out to the master, he not only came to their defense, but replied with a forthright aggression that seems more violent than the case merits. Jesus seized the opportunity to elucidate an important point. His replies were not so revolutionary as the uninitiated might imagine. His saying about purity and impurity is almost a piece of popular moral wisdom, and the kernel of Jesus' saying in the debate about plucking ears of corn on the sabbath is completely in harmony with the views of the moderate scribes. On that occasion, Jesus said—among other things: "The sabbath was made for man, not man for the sabbath; so the Son of man is Lord even of the sabbath" (Mk. 2:27–28). The scribes, too, said: "The sabbath has been handed over to you, not you to the sabbath."[55]

Jesus, too, knew how to seize suitable opportunities for his pedagogic attacks upon the hypocrites. He did this, for example,

Curing the lame man. From the church in Dura Europos, first half of the third century.

when he performed a miracle of healing on the sabbath. To understand the way this worked out, we have to know that if there was even a slight suspicion of danger to life, any form of healing was permitted. Nonetheless, mechanical means were not allowed; but healing by word was always permitted on the sabbath, even when the illness was not dangerous. According to the synoptic gospels, Jesus always conformed to these rules in all of his healings.[56] Not so with John, who was less interested in history. He reports the healing of the blind man, a story that is reminiscent of Mark 8:22–26. According to John 9:6, Jesus healed the man by placing mud made from earth and spittle on the blind man's eyes. In contrast to Mark, John adds: "Now it was a sabbath day when Jesus made clay and opened his eyes . . . Some of the Pharisees said, 'This man is not from God, for he

49

does not keep the sabbath' " (Jn. 9:14–16). If Jesus had acted thus, the objection of the Pharisees would have made sense from their point of view; but as we have said, Jesus had no desire to oppose the law of Moses. He only wanted to expose the blindness of the hypocrites, using this case as an example. He knew how to create opportunities to do this. "On another sabbath, when he entered the synagogue and taught, a man was there whose right hand was withered. And they watched him, to see whether he would heal on the sabbath, so that they might find an accusation against him. But he said to them: 'Is it lawful to do good on the sabbath?' And he said to the man: 'Stretch out your hand.' And he did so, and his hand was restored like the other. But they were at a loss and asked one another: 'What are we to do with Jesus?' " (Lk. 6:6–11).

Jesus, already known to be a healer, meets a man with a withered hand in the synagogue on the sabbath. The man is chronically, not dangerously, ill. Is Jesus going to heal this man? Yes, but by using words only, as was permitted. By this deed, and by what he said, he had shown the true meaning of the sabbath. Naturally, he roused the sanctimonious people who had been unable to catch him out breaking the law. In the original account, moreover, the Pharisees were not explicitly mentioned.[57] This plain fact was then distorted by Mark, for no reason at all, and Matthew followed Mark. In Mark, the story ends not with the impotent confusion of the hypocrites, but in this way: "The Pharisees went out, and immediately held counsel with the Herodians against him, how to destroy him." This is a plain reference to the coming crucifixion (cf. Mk. 15:1). It is most unlikely that the Pharisees would have acted in that way. The most wicked among them would never have resolved to kill Jesus because he had performed a work of healing on the sabbath—a permissible deed anyway. For this reason Luke's version (6:11) is preferable here.

Jesus, then, emphasized the moral side of life in preference to the purely formal side of legal observance. We can give a little more depth to this provisional affirmation by leaving the

Inscription from an ancient synagogue in Jerusalem.

question of the law and going on to mention two other controversial conversations of Jesus. The first has the same polemical overtone as the saying on the occasion of the healing of the withered hand. "And behold, they brought to him a paralytic, lying on his bed; and when Jesus saw their faith he said: 'My son, your sins are forgiven.' And behold, some of the scribes said to themselves: 'This man is blaspheming. Who can forgive sins but God?' But Jesus, knowing their thoughts, said: 'What are you thinking in your hearts? For which is easier, to say, "Your sins are forgiven," or to say, "Rise and walk"? But that you may know that man[58] has authority on earth to forgive sins'—he then said to the paralytic: 'Rise, take up your bed and go home.' And he rose and went home. And all were afraid, and they glorified God, who had given such authority to men" (cf. Mt. 9:1–8).

As in the healing of the withered hand, in this healing, too, Jesus links word with deed. The healing was not an end in itself, but a striking proof of a doctrine. Because people believed that illnesses were a consequence of sins committed, forgive-

51

ness of sins can even imply healing. By healing the paralytic, Jesus proved that God had given power to men, in their own strength, to forgive sins that had no connection at all with the one who forgave. It is also important that Jesus forgave the sick man his sins after having perceived the faith of those present, and also, apparently, the faith of the sick man. The original account makes no mention of belief in Jesus himself—it became taken for granted in the Christian era—but the power of faith itself was already recognized by Jesus. "If you have faith as a grain of mustard seed, you will say to this mountain, 'Move hence to yonder place,' and it will move" (Mt. 17:20).

The other controversy, too, was about the forgiveness of sins. It was alleged that Jesus' healing power came from Beelzebub, the prince of spirits, by whose power Jesus drove out the spirits. One of his replies to this calumny is reported in Mt. 12:32: "And whoever says a word against the Son of man will be forgiven; but whoever speaks against the Holy Spirit will not be forgiven, either in this age or the age to come." The real significance of this saying, which has parallels in Jewish writings,[59] lies in the fact that, since his baptism, Jesus knew he possessed the Holy Spirit. It is important also because it shows us the substance to which Jesus is pointing in his controversies, even in those concerned with the observance of the law: man, his sins, and his authority.

In the course of oral and written tradition, the protagonists in Jesus' controversial dialogues become more sharply delineated —and increasingly distorted. In the original account Jesus' opponents are often anonymous self-appointed spokesmen of local bigotry; later they are described unhesitatingly as scribes and Pharisees.[60] It is worthwhile following the progressive development of the text in order to see how Jesus' opponents increasingly become his enemies, inspired by boundless wickedness, having as their ultimate goal his overthrow and destruction.

There is some justification, however, in describing Jesus' opponents-in-argument as Pharisees. In the narrower sense, the

Pharisees were a society whose members—as we said—had voluntarily accepted certain prescriptions of purity, and other obligations. In Jesus' time, this society numbered about six thousand members. They were founded in the second century before Christ, in a turbulent period when they had been the opponents of the Maccabean ruling dynasty, which had made alliance with the politico-religious movement of the Sadducees, and they had developed throughout the civil wars. The outcome was that by Jesus' time the Sadducees formed a small but powerful group among the priestly aristocracy of the temple in Jerusalem, whereas the Pharisees had become the teachers of the mass of the people. They had succeeded in acquiring this office by consciously identifying themselves with popular faith. Fundamentally, the Pharisaic philosophy of life was in line with non-sectarian universal Judaism, whereas the Sadducees, by contrast, had turned into a counter-revolutionary group. They denied the validity of oral tradition and saw belief in a future life as an old wives' tale. The Pharisees were not identical with the scribes, the later rabbis; but the two groups may, in practice, be regarded as forming a unity.

We know two men who called themselves Pharisees: the historian, Flavius Josephus,[61] and St. Paul,[62] and neither of them was typical of Pharisaism. In their writings, they scarcely described the rabbis as Pharisees. For example, St. Paul's teacher, Rabbi Gamaliel, is called a Pharisee only in Acts 5:34; and his son, Simon, is thus described only in Josephus.[63] The reason for this is, in part at least, that the term "Pharisee" usually bore a negative connotation.

In those days, if one said, "Pharisee," one immediately thought of a religious hypocrite. On his deathbed the Sadducean King Alexander Jannaeus warned his wife not against the true Pharisees, but against the "painted ones, whose deeds are the deeds of Zimri, but who expect to receive the reward[64] of Phinehas."[65] The Sadducean king spoke of "the painted ones," the Essenes called the Pharisees "the whitewashed,"[66] and Jesus said: "Woe to you, scribes and Pharisees, hypocrites! for you are like white-

Left: Coin of Alexander Jannaeus, 103–76 B.C.
Right: The seven-branched candlestick. Coin of Mattathias Antigonus, 40–37 B.C.

washed tombs, which outwardly appear beautiful, but within they are full of dead men's bones and all uncleanness. So you also outwardly appear righteous to men, but within you are full of hypocrisy and iniquity" (Mt. 23:27–28). The Sadducean king distinguished between the wicked deeds of the "whitewashed" and their claim to be honored as righteous. The Essenes, too, condemned the deeds of the Pharisees: "And they lead thy people astray, for they utter smooth speeches to them. False teachers, they lead astray, and blindly they are heading for a fall, for their works are done in deceit."[67] Jesus saw the hypocrisy of the Pharisees in the discrepancy between their doctrine and their deeds, "for they preach, but do not practise" (Mt. 23:3).

It is worth noting that this same anti-Pharisaic polemic occurs also in rabbinic literature, which is an expression of true Pharisaism. The talmudic list of the seven kinds of Pharisee[68] is a fivefold variation on the theme of hypocrisy—the last two kinds of hypocrisy are replaced by two positive kinds of Pharisee. It is thus no accident that in the Pharisee discourse of Mt. 23:1–36, Jesus addresses seven "Woes" to the Pharisees. The first type in the talmudic list is the "shoulder-Pharisee who lays commandments upon men's shoulders";[69] and Jesus likewise said that the

54

Ossuary from the environs of Jerusalem.

Pharisees "bind heavy burdens, hard to bear, and lay them on men's shoulders; but they themselves will not move them with their finger" (Mt. 23:4).

The Essene writings are full of the bitterest attacks upon the party of the Pharisees—although the name is not directly mentioned. The Pharisees were described as "slippery exponents," their actions were hypocrisy and by means of "their deceitful doctrine, lying tongues and false lips" they were able to lead almost the whole people astray.[70] In all this, "they closed up the fountain of knowledge to the thirsty and gave them vinegar with which to quench their thirst."[71] This reminds us of Jesus' words: "Woe to your lawyers! for you have taken away the key of knowledge; you did not enter yourselves, and you hindered those who were entering" (Lk. 11:52; cf. Mt. 23:13). Nevertheless, the gap between the Essene attack upon the Pharisees and Jesus' criticism of them is very big. The Essenes sharply rejected the doctrine of the Pharisees, whereas Jesus said: "The scribes and Pharisees sit on Moses' seat; so practise and observe whatever they tell you, but not what they do; for they preach, but do not practise" (Mt. 23:2–3).

In the Pharisees Jesus saw the contemporary heirs of Moses,

and said that men should model their lives upon their teaching. This makes sense, for although Jesus was apparently indirectly influenced by Essenism, he was basically rooted in universal non-sectarian Judaism, and the philosophy and practice of this Judaism was that of the Pharisees. Yet it would be wrong to describe Jesus simply as a Pharisee in the broad sense. Even if his criticism of the Pharisees was not so hostile as was that of the Essenes, nor so contradictory as that of the contemporary literature we have cited, he did view the Pharisees with detachment, as it were, and refused to identify himself with them. We have still to discuss the inevitable tension between the charismatic miracles of Jesus, and institutional Judaism; nor dare we forget that the revolutionary element in his preaching of the kingdom heightened this tension. It will become evident also that the authentic teaching of Jesus questioned the foundations of the social structure as such; but all of this did not turn tension into contradiction, nor did it degenerate into enmity.

Even were it not possible to strip off the retouching of our sources by the application of philological method, it would be very difficult to understand the existence of the scribes' and Pharisees' genuine hostility towards Jesus—allegedly a contributory cause of his death. Obviously, there were some petty minds among the Pharisees—such people are found in all societies—who were suspicious of this wonder-worker, and who would gladly have caught him in some forbidden action so that they could drag him before the rabbinic court; but Jesus always succeeded in stating his opinion without giving them the slightest excuse for prosecuting him. Those who know the scribes of those days are well aware that their leaders were not without faults; but they know also that they were far from being petty-minded.

If Jesus had lived in the stormy days of the last Maccabean kings, it would certainly have been possible for him to have been persecuted by the Pharisees, because he was the leader of a Messianic movement. When the Pharisees came to power under Queen Salome Alexandra, by no means did they spare their Sadducean opponents; and the Dead Sea scrolls tell us that they

The chair of Moses from an ancient synagogue in Galilee. Archaeological Museum, Jerusalem.

also unleashed a regular persecution against the Essenes. But all that belonged to a past of which the Pharisees were ashamed. Jesus has something fine to say on this topic: "Woe to you, scribes and Pharisees, hypocrites! for you build the tombs of the prophets and adorn the monuments of the righteous, saying, 'If we had lived in the days of our fathers, we would not have taken part with them in shedding the blood of prophets.' Thus you witness against yourselves, that you are the sons of those who murdered the prophets" (Mt. 23:29–31).[72]

The testimonial which Jesus has involuntarily given the

Ancient Jewish sepulchres in Jerusalem.

Pharisees of his time is confirmed by the report of the trial of Jesus. It is hardly ever pointed out that the Pharisees, so often mentioned in the gospels as Jesus' opponents, do not appear in any of the synoptic accounts of the trial. The fact that it would have been very easy to smuggle the word "Pharisees" into these relatively late accounts is proved by the less historical John, who had no qualms over writing thus of Jesus' arrest: "So Judas, procuring a band of soldiers and some officers from the chief priests and the Pharisees, went there with lanterns and torches and weapons" (Jn. 18:3).

The reason why not only the original accounts, but the three first gospels, avoid mentioning the Pharisees in the story of the trial of Jesus, becomes clearer if we recall the role of the Pharisees in the first decades of the Christian Church. When the apostles were persecuted by the Sadducean high priest, the Rabbi Gamaliel took their part and saved them (Acts 5:17–42). When Paul was taken before the high council in Jerusalem, he got off

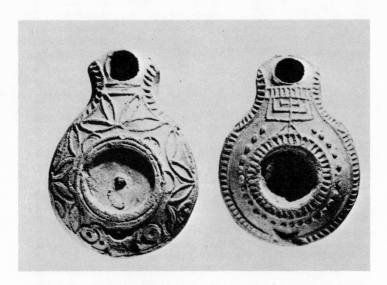

Jewish lamps of the Roman period. The right lamp depicts the seven-branched candlestick.

with his life by appealing to the Pharisees (Acts 22:30—23:10). When in 62 A.D., the Lord's brother James, and apparently other Christians, were illegally put to death by the Sadducean High Priest, the Pharisees appealed to the king, and the High Priest was deposed.[73]

Taking the last case along with the two earlier ones, we can hardly avoid the impression that the Pharisees regarded the Sadducean priestly aristocracy's persecution of the early Christians as further proof of the manifestly unjust cruelty of this group, and that out of it they forged a moral-political weapon against the Sadducean priesthood—politics is not always an evil business. This explains the Pharisees' apparently consistent opposition to the persecutions of the Christians by the Sadducean high priests, one of whom lost his office as a result of this opposition. The reason why the early Christians became a bone of contention between the two Jewish parties is that the Pharisees regarded the handing over of Jesus to the Romans as an act of high priestly

59

A page from the biblical manuscript, Codex Aleppo. From the Book of Deuteronomy.

despotism. We can assume also that the Pharisees do not figure as accusers of Jesus at his trial in the first three gospel accounts because at that time—in the eighties of the first century—people knew that the Pharisees had not agreed to hand Jesus over to the Romans. Probably, the synoptists could not name the Pharisees as present at the trial; had they done so, people would not have believed their report. The synoptists could not mention the protest of the Pharisees either, because they had already portrayed Jesus as an anti-Pharisee in the earlier part of their narratives.

How curious the changes a movement can undergo in the course of its history! As early as the second century, Christians of Jewish origin, who continued to follow the law of Moses, were being penalized,[74] and later, all Christians were forbidden to keep the precepts of the old covenant, although Jesus had said: "For truly, I say to you, till heaven and earth pass away, not an iota, not a dot, will pass from the law[75] until all is accomplished. Whoever then relaxes one of the least of these commandments and teaches men so, shall be called least in the kingdom of heaven; but he who does them and teaches them shall be called great in the kingdom of heaven" (Mt. 5:18–20).

The abrogation of the Jewish laws within the Church is connected therefore, with the fact, that meanwhile Christianity had been turning into a non-Jewish religion. It was possible for this to happen, because in the ancient world, very many people regarded the God of the Jews as the one true God. Hence, there were many men in those days who took the final step, and became fully converted to Judaism. The liberal school of Hillel was not unhappy to see Gentiles becoming Jews; but, in contrast, the school of Shammai made this conversion as difficult as possible. The following sayings show that Jesus shared the strict standpoint of Shammai. "Woe to you, scribes and Pharisees, hypocrites! for you traverse sea and land to make a single proselyte, and when he becomes a proselyte, you make him twice as much a child of hell as yourselves" (Mt. 23:15). A non-Jew who lives according to certain fundamental moral laws, without following the whole Mosaic law, is blessed. The proselyte, the Gentile who has turned Jew, however, is bound by the whole law. If a proselyte fails to fulfill the law perfectly—which formerly did not obligate him—his conversion to Judaism is itself the cause of his becoming a child of hell; quite needlessly he has thrown away his blessedness.

As far as the sources allow us to judge, Jesus had a poor opinion of the non-Jews, the Gentiles.[76] They are anxious about their material future and do not know that "tomorrow will be anxious for itself" (Mt. 6:33–34); they "heap up empty phrases" in prayer, thinking "that they will be heard for their many words" (Mt. 6:7); they know nothing of the Jews' command to love

61

one's neighbor and mix only with their friends (Mt. 5:47). The first and the third sayings give us the feeling that Jesus is speaking about the vices that still afflict European society to some extent. There is another very profound saying which seems directed chiefly against the Romans. When the disciples were disputing about who was the greatest among them, Jesus said to them: "The rulers of the Gentiles lord it over them; it shall not be so among you; the great among you must be the lesser, and the first like a slave. For the Son of man came not to be served but to serve" (Mt. 20:24–28).[77] Jesus' saying is a profound reinterpretation of the biblical saying: "The elder shall serve the younger" (Gen. 25:23). This was a prophecy of the waning power of the elder Esau under the ascendancy of the younger Jacob. In Jesus' time Esau was taken as symbolizing Rome. Jesus is saying, therefore, that the Roman rulers of the nations have power over them, but for us the biblical words mean that the greater shall serve the lesser, for that is what man is here to do.

What has been said makes it plain, therefore, why Jesus commanded the twelve: "Go nowhere among the Gentiles, and enter no town of the Samaritans, but go rather to the lost sheep of the house of Israel" (Mt. 10:5–6).[78] These words of Jesus refer presumably not merely to preaching to non-Jews, but also to healing, which was one of the functions of the disciples. At all events Jesus as a rule did not heal non-Jews. On one occasion a Syro-Phoenician woman entreated him to heal her mentally ill daughter, and he reiterated what he had said to his disciples: "I was sent only to the lost sheep of the house of Israel." But she came and knelt before him, saying, "Lord, help me." And he answered, "It is not fair to take the children's bread and throw it to the dogs." She said, "Yes, Lord, even the dogs eat the crumbs that fall from their master's table." Jesus was moved by what the woman said and her daughter was healed from that hour (Mt. 15:21–28).

There is only one more report of Jesus healing a non-Jew: the servant of the Roman centurion at Capernaum (Mt. 8:5–13;

A portrait from a grave near Ascalon, c. 300 A.D.

Lk. 7:1–10). Luke tells us that the centurion was no heathen, but a man who feared God. He said to Jesus: "Lord . . . I am not worthy to have you come under my roof; . . . but say the word, and let my servant be healed." This devout Roman wanted to avoid the possibility of Jesus contracting impurity through contact with a non-Jew, and so he asked Jesus to heal his servant from a distance. He based his belief in the power of this wonder-working Rabbi Jesus to heal in this way, upon a comparison with his own office: " 'For I am a man set under authority, with soldiers under me: and I say to one, "Go," and he goes; and to another, "Come," and he comes; and to my slave, "Do this," and he does it.' When Jesus heard this he marvelled at him, and turned and said to the multitude that followed him, 'I tell you,

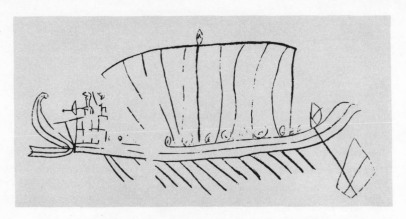

Ship. Drawing from a Jewish grave, beginning of the first century B.C.

not even in Israel have I found such faith.' " At that hour the servant was healed.

These are the only two stories in which Jesus healed a non-Jew. In both the decisive words are spoken not by Jesus, but by the heathen, and these words make a deep impression on Jesus. We ought to notice also that none of the rabbinical documents say that one should not or may not heal a non-Jew.

The picture preserved for us by the first three gospels is clear: Jesus, the Jew, worked among Jews and wanted to work only among them. Even Paul, apostle of the Gentiles, confirms this fact: Jesus was "born under the law" (Gal. 4:4); he was "a servant to the circumcised to show God's truthfulness, in order to confirm the promises given to the patriarchs" (Rom. 15:8).

Were the various Jewish-Christian sects right then in thinking that by living as Jews they were following the will of Jesus? Expelled from the synagogues as heretics, stigmatized by the Catholic Church as unorthodox, these Jews lived by the firm conviction that they alone cherished the true heritage of their master, and that thereby they too happened to be the only ones who grasped the true meaning of Judaism. History passed them by; they became embittered; and so among them the preaching of Jesus gradually turned into a rigid apologetic caricature. As late as the tenth century they are to be found somewhere in Mossul,[79] utterly lonely in their superhuman loyalty.

64

LOVE

The germ of revolution—if we may speak thus—in Jesus' preaching does not emerge from a criticism of the Jewish law, but from other premises altogether. Jesus was not the first to provide these: his attack proceeded from attitudes already established before his time. Revolution broke through at three points: the radical commandment of love, the call for a new morality, the idea of the kingdom of heaven.

In about the year 175 B.C. a Jewish scribe bearing the Greek name Antigonos of Ssocho used to say: "Be not like slaves who serve their master for the sake of reward, but like slaves who serve their master with no eye on any reward; and may the fear of heaven be among you."[80] This saying is characteristic of the change in intellectual and moral atmosphere that had taken place in Judaism since the time of the Old Testament.[81] At the same time, it is the expression of a new and deeper sensitivity within Judaism, which was an important precondition for the preaching of Jesus.

The religion of Israel preached the one righteous God: his iconoclastic exclusiveness was linked with his inflexible moral will. The righteousness of the Old Testament seeks concrete expression in a new and just social order. God's righteousness is also his compassion; he espouses especially the cause of the poor and oppressed, for he desires not men's physical power and strength, but their fear of him. The Jewish religion is a religion of morality in which the principle of justice is indispensable. That is why the division of men into just and sinners is so important. For the Jew, the concept that God rewards the just and punishes the wicked is the confirmation of God's steadfast truth. How, otherwise, could the righteousness of God prevail in the world?

Man's destiny, however, seldom corresponds to his moral endeavor; often guilt obviously goes unpunished, and virtue unrewarded. It is thus easy for man to see that something is amiss; but no ethics and no religion has yet succeeded in solving the problem of evil. In the Old Testament, the book of Job is devoted to the topic of the bitter lot of the righteous; and Eastern heathen wisdom literature too knows the cry: "They walk on a lucky path those who do not seek a god. Those who devoutly pray to a goddess become poor and weak."[82]

It was not this problem that caused the revolution that led to the moral imperative of Jesus. As we have said, the moral-religious maxim according to which the righteous flourish and the evil come to a bad end, is constantly refuted by life. For the Jew of ancient times, however, the statement was doubtful from another point of view also. Even if the maxim had been confirmed by experience, the question would still have to be asked: Is the simple division of men into righteous and sinners itself appropriate? We know, it is true, that no one is perfectly just or utterly evil, for good and evil struggle within the heart of every man. Also, there arises the question of the limits of the mercy of God and of his love for men. Even if there were no problems about the reward of the just and the punishment of the sinner, would a man be performing a truly moral act if he performed it because he knew that he would be rewarded? As we have said, Antigonos of Ssocho believed this to be the morality of the slave: a man ought to act morally, and at the same time give no thought to the reward that will surely come to him.

The black and white morality of the old covenant was clearly inadequate for the new sensitivity of the Jews of classical times. Having now recognized that men are not sharply divided into righteous and sinners, it was practically impossible for one to love the good and hate the wicked. Because it had become difficult to know how far God's love and mercy extended, many concluded that one ought to show love and mercy towards one's neighbor, thus imitating God himself. Luke 6:36 puts this saying into the mouth of Jesus: "Be merciful, even as your Father is merciful." This is an old rabbinical saying.[83]

In those circles where, at that time, the new Jewish sensitivity was especially well developed, love of one's neighbor was regarded as a precondition of reconciliation with God. "Transgressions between a man and his neighbor are not expiated by the Day of Atonement unless the man first makes peace with his neighbor." Thus spoke a rabbi a few years after Jesus.[84] And Jesus said: "For if you forgive men their trespasses, your heavenly Father also will forgive you; but if you do not forgive men their trespasses, neither will your Father forgive your trespasses" (Mt. 6:14–15).

The best summary of the new Jewish ethics is found in its oldest manifesto, Ecclesiasticus, or the Wisdom of Jesus the Son of Sirach (27:30—28:7), which was written about the year 185 B.C.

> "Anger and wrath, these also are abominations, and the sinful man will possess them.
> He that takes vengeance will suffer vengeance from the Lord, and he will firmly establish his sins.
> Forgive your neighbor the wrong he has done, and then your sins will be pardoned when you pray.
> Does a man harbor anger against another, and yet seek for healing from the Lord?
> Does he have no mercy towards a man like himself, and yet pray for his own sins?
> If he himself, being flesh, maintains wrath, who will make expiations for his sins?
> Remember the end of your life, and cease from enmity, remember destruction and death, and be true to the commandments.
> Remember the commandments, and do not be angry with your neighbor; remember the covenant of the Most High, and overlook ignorance."

The notion we have already encountered, that a man must be reconciled with his brother before praying for himself, is linked in Sirach with a modification of the old idea of reward that is typical of the period. The old compensatory justice whereby the righteous was rewarded according to the measure of his righteousness, and the sinner punished according to the measure of his sins, filled many in those days with uneasiness; and so, they began to think: if you love your neighbor, God will reward you with good; if you hate your neighbor, God will visit you with evil. Jesus too said something like this: "Judge not, and you will not be judged; condemn not and you will not be condemned; forgive, and you will be forgiven; give, and it will be given to you; good measure, pressed down, shaken together, running over, will be put into your lap. For the measure you give will be the measure you get back" (Lk. 6:37–38).

The beginning of this saying reminds us of the saying of the celebrated Hillel who had already said: "Judge not your neighbor lest you find yourself in his place!"[85] The saying: "The measure you give will be the measure you get back" was a proverb among the Jews in those days.[86] The saying of Jesus reported by Luke finds an important parallel in the Lord's words as reproduced by Clement of Rome about 96 A.D.: "Be merciful, and you will find mercy; forgive, and you will be forgiven; as you do, so it will be done to you; as you give, so it will be given to you; as you judge, so you will be judged; as you do good, so will good be done to you; with the same measure in which you give, it will be given to you" (1 *Clem.* 13:2). This saying came from the early Church or perhaps from Jesus himself.[87]

The themes in which the new sensitivity in Judaism expressed itself in those days were closely interwoven. These themes interrelate many of the sayings of Jesus, and also relate his sayings with many Jewish proverbs. Thus Clement of Rome reports the Lord as saying: "as you do, so it will be done to you," that is to say, as you treat your neighbor, so God will treat you. This is a most interesting variation on the so-called Golden Rule accepted as a moral imperative by many nations, and amongst the Jews;[88] even before the time of Jesus, it was regarded as the sum of all the law. Hillel had said: "What is distasteful to yourself, do not do to your neighbor; that is the whole law, the rest is but commentary." The Jews of that time probably put this interpretation upon the maxim also: God metes out to you in the same measure in which you mete out to your neighbor. The conclusion follows: "As a man pleads before God for his own soul, so should he plead for every living soul."[89]

Both Jesus and Hillel before him saw the Golden Rule as a summary of the law of Moses. This becomes intelligible when we consider that the biblical saying: "you shall love your neighbor as yourself" (Lev. 19:18) was esteemed by Jesus and by the Jews in general as a great chief commandment of the law.[90] An old Aramaic translation of this biblical precept runs like this: "Love your neighbor, for whatever displeases you, do not to him!" This paraphrastic translation turns the phrase "as yourself" into the negative style of the Golden Rule. The saying: "Love your neighbor" was understood as a positive commandment, and the words "as yourself" as a negative commandment included in it: you are not to treat your neighbor with hatred, because you would not like him to treat you in that way. Therefore, by means of Jewish parallels we have been able to see how the Golden Rule (Mt. 7:12) and the commandment to love our neighbor (Mt. 22:39) are related within Jesus' teaching.

There was yet another explanation of the phrase "as yourself" in the biblical commandment to love one's neighbor, so important in those days. In Hebrew the phrase can also mean "as though he were yourself." The commandment then reads: "Love your neighbor for he is like yourself." Sirach knew of this interpretation when he demanded that one forgive one's neighbor his trespasses, for it is a sin to withhold mercy from "a man like himself" (Sir. 28:3–5). Rabbi Hanina, who lived approximately one generation after Jesus, explicitly taught that this commandment to love one's neighbor is: "A saying upon which the whole world hangs, a mighty oath from Mount Sinai. If you hate your neighbor whose deeds are wicked like your own, I, the Lord, will punish you as your judge; and if you love your neighbor whose deeds are good like your own, I, the Lord, will be faithful to you and have mercy on you."[91] A man's relationship to his neighbor ought, therefore, to be determined by the fact that he is one with him both in his good and in his evil characteristics. This is not far from Jesus' commandment to love; but Jesus went further and broke the last fetters still restricting the ancient Jewish commandment to love one's neighbor. Rabbi Hanina believed that one ought to love the righteous and not to hate the sinner, but Jesus said: "I say to you, Love your enemies and pray for those who persecute you" (Mt. 5:44).

We shall see, it is true, that in those days the semi-Essene circles had reached similar conclusions from different presuppositions, and that Jesus' moral teaching was influenced by these circles also; but influences do not explain everything. He who avoided his parental home in Nazareth and became the "friend of publicans and sinners" felt himself sent to "the lost sheep of the house of Israel." It was not simply his total picture of life that urged Jesus on to loving devotion to sinners: this inclination was deeply linked with the purpose of his message. Moreover, from his infancy until his death on the cross the preaching of Jesus was, in turn, linked with his total picture of life. The commandment to love one's enemies is so much his definitive characteristic that his are the only lips from which we hear the commandment in the whole of the New Testament. Elsewhere we hear only of mutual love and blessing one's persecutors. In those days it was obviously very difficult for people to rise up to the heights of Jesus' commandment.

Jesus mentioned the biblical commandment when he was explaining the sum and substance of the law of Moses: " 'Teacher, which is the great commandment in the law?' And he said to him, 'You shall love the Lord your God with all your heart, and with all your soul, and with all your mind (Dt. 6:5). This is the great and first commandment. And the second is like it, You shall love your neighbor as yourself (Lev. 19:18). On these two commandments depend all the law and the prophets' " (Mt. 22:35–40).[92]

It is almost certain that here Jesus was teaching a proverb of oral tradition because he saw it as important for his own message. This happened on other occasions too: he simply took over a saying of some scribe. "And he said to them, 'Therefore every scribe[93] who has been trained for the kingdom of heaven is like a householder who brings out of his treasure what is new and what is old'" (Mt. 13:52). Jesus' saying about the double commandment of love clearly was coined before the time of Jesus. We have already seen that the biblical saying about love of one's neighbor was also described elsewhere as "the great commandment in the law,"[94] and this commandment is truly like the other—the commandment to love God—for both verses from the Bible (Dt. 6:5 and Lev. 19:18) begin with the same phrase. It was typical of rabbinical scholarship to see similarly phrased passages from the Bible as connected in content also. The first great commandment of Jesus—love of God—was thus in harmony with the spirit of contemporary Pharisaism.[95] In the list of the seven kinds of Pharisee which we have already mentioned,[96] two positive types are named: the Pharisee of fear like Job and the Pharisee of love like Abraham. The many rabbinical documents which compare fear of God and love of God set love much higher than fear, for it was in harmony with the new Jewish sensitivity to serve God out of unconditional love rather than out of fear of punishment.[97]

All that has been said explains how the double commandment of love existed in ancient Judaism before, and alongside Jesus.[98] The fact that it does not appear in the rabbinical documents that have come down to us is probably a sheer accident; for Mark (12:28–34) and Luke (10:25–28) show that on the question of "the great commandment" Jesus and the scribes were in agreement.

The saying before us is but one example of many in which the uninitiated reader thinks he finds a specially characteristic teaching of Jesus, and in so doing fails to observe the significance of the really revolutionary sayings. All the same, such sayings as the great commandment fulfill a significant function within the total preaching of Jesus. From ancient Jewish writings we could easily construct a whole gospel without using a single word that originated with Jesus. This could only be done, however, because we do in fact possess the gospels.

The same is true of the section of the Sermon on the Mount in which Jesus allegedly defines his own personal attitude towards the law of Moses (Mt. 5:17–48). There, so to speak, he brings things old and new out of his treasure.

The sensitivity of ancient Judaism evolved, in contrast to the simple view of the Old Testament, a whole dialectic of sin; for when man ceases to be regarded as an unproblematical being, sins themselves become a problem. If a man is not careful, one sin can lead to another; and even an action that does not appear sinful can cause a man to become entangled in a real sin. There was a saying: "Flee from what is evil and from what resembles evil." If we apply this concept to the commandments, we discover that the lesser commandments are as serious as the greater.

Jesus' exegesis in Mt. 5:17–48 should be understood in this sense also. The exegesis proper is preceded by a preamble (Mt. 5:17–20) in which Jesus justifies his method. It would seem that exaggerated importance has been attached to the first sentence (Mt. 5:17) of this introduction. Jesus only seemed to say: "Think not that I have come to abolish the law;[99] I have come not to abolish, but to fulfill," and thus, following the customary language[100] of his time, he avoided the reproach that the exegesis of the law which followed abrogated the original meaning of the words of the Bible. He could not have wanted to do this because the law, as written, is mysteriously bound up with the existence of this world; so, even the minor commandments are to be obeyed. This implies a tightening up of the law, not in respect of ritual, but in respect of the relationships between man and man. This attitude was present in contemporary Judaism too, as the following saying exemplifies: "Everyone who publicly shames his neighbor sheds his blood."[101] The first two biblical exegeses of Jesus in the Sermon on the Mount are constructed on this conceptual and formal scheme: it is not just the murderer, but he who is angry with his brother, who is condemned (Mt. 5:21–22), and "every one who looks at a woman lustfully has already committed adultery with her in his heart" (Mt. 5:28). According to a later traditional Jewish saying[102] three classes of sinners are consigned to hell for all eternity: the adulterer, he who publicly puts his neighbor to shame, and he who insults his neighbor. Jesus, too, had something to say on this last type: "Whoever insults his brother shall be liable to the council, and whoever says, 'You fool!' shall be liable to hell" (Mt. 5:22). The continuation (Mt. 5:29–30) has an interesting parallel in rabbinical literature. Jesus said (cf. Mk. 9:43–48):[103] "If your eye causes you to sin, pluck it out, for it is better to lose it than for your whole body to go into hell." The same is said about the hand and the foot. Earlier (Mt. 5:28) Jesus said that every one who had looked at a woman lustfully had already committed adultery with her in his heart. There was a Jewish opinion[104] that the word "to commit adultery" in Hebrew had four letters in order to warn us that adultery could be committed by hand, foot, eye, and heart.

Jesus began his exegesis of the scriptures by stressing the importance of the lesser commandments. In this spirit he is then able to equate anger with murder and lust with adultery. In the Jewish "Two Ways" which is preserved in the early Christian document[105] the *Didache,* we read: "My child, flee all evil, and from all that is like unto it. Be not soon angry, for anger leadeth to murder, . . . My child, be not lustful, for lust leadeth to fornication, . . . for from all these are generated adulteries."[106] We have already met the first statement as a Jewish moral rule, and the two applications of the rule correspond to the sixth and the seventh of the ten commandments which Jesus expounds in exactly the same way in the Sermon on the Mount. In this the second table of the Decalogue can be seen in the background of Jesus' scriptural exegesis, and it is seen even more clearly in the "Two Ways." These biblical commandments speak of our relation to our neighbor, and so the real conclusion of Jesus' exegesis is his commentary (Mt. 5:43–48) on the great commandment, "Love your neighbor as yourself."

Those who listened to Jesus' preaching of love might well have been moved by it. Many in those days thought as he did. Nonetheless, in the clear purity of his love they must have detected something very special. Jesus did not accept all that was thought and taught in the Judaism of his time. Although not really a Pharisee himself, he was closest to the Pharisees of the school of Hillel who preached love, but he pointed the way further to unconditional love—even of one's enemies and of sinners. As we shall see, this was no sentimental doctrine.

A deer. Drawing from a Jewish grave, beginning of the first century B.C.

MORALITY

One day someone said to Jesus: "I will follow you wherever you go." The reply was: "Foxes have holes, and the birds of the air have nests; but the Son of man[107] has nowhere to lay his head" (Mt. 8:19–20). This saying constitutes a social protest. The American negro social outcasts know well what Jesus meant, when they sing:

> De foxes have holes in de groun',
> An de birds have nests in de air,
> An ev'ryting have a hiding place,
> But we poor sinners have none.[108]

With Jesus, the social overtone is louder than with the rabbis; it forms the core of his authentic message. However, Jesus was no social revolutionary in the usual sense of the word. The Essenes were of a different stamp. Originally they had been an apocalyptic revolutionary movement whose ideology of poverty was combined with the doctrine of double predestination. They, the true sons of light, the divinely chosen poor, by the power of arms and the assistance of the heavenly hosts, would soon, at the imminent end of time, inherit the land and conquer the whole world. The sons of darkness, the rest of Israel, and the Gentiles, along with the demonic powers who rule the world, would then be annihilated. Even if in Jesus' time, their ideology was probably no longer so activist, and the Essenes had become a more contemplative mystic sect, they still lived in communities with common ownership, prized poverty highly, and kept themselves strictly apart from the rest of Jewish society.

The Essene sons of light restricted to the minimum economic links with the surrounding world. "None of them will eat of their food or drink of their drink or take anything from their hands, unless it has been bought from them . . . for, . . . all who despise His word He will recompense out of the world, all their deeds are as filth before Him, and all their possessions are stained with uncleanness."[109] The Essenes, then, were obliged "to cut themselves off from the sons of destruction and keep free from the impure possession of profanity."[110]

Obviously, Jesus was unable to assent to this ideological and economic separation of the Essenes. "The sons of this world are wiser in their own generation than the children of light. And I tell you, make friends for yourself by[111] means of unrighteous mammon[112] . . . If then you have not been faithful in the unrighteous mammon, who will entrust to you the true riches? And if you have not been faithful in that which is another's, who will give you that which is your own?" (Lk. 16:8–12). Jesus must have known the Essenes, therefore, and with a dash of irony alluded to them, using their own self-description—"sons of light."

Like the Essenes of his own time, Jesus too regarded all possessions as a threat to true piety. "No one can serve two masters; for either he will hate the one and love the other, or he will be devoted to the one and despise the other. You cannot serve God and mammon" (Mt. 6:24). The dualism of this saying is Essene in outlook: the Essenes endeavoured "to love everything that he has chosen, to hate everything that he has repudiated, to keep far from evil, and cleave to all good works."[113] Between good and evil there is eternal enmity, and so also between the sons of light and the sons of darkness, between God and Belial, the devil. Jesus could not accept this attitude; he did not take over Essene theology, but only certain social consequences of their philosophy of life. Therefore, the two masters who figure in his saying are not God and the devil, Belial, but God and mammon.

According to Jesus, possessions are an obstacle to virtue. "Children, how hard it is for those who trust in riches to enter the kingdom of God! It is easier for a camel to go through the eye of a needle than for a rich man to enter the kingdom of God" (Mk. 10:24–25). For both the Essenes and Jesus, therefore, poverty, humility, purity of heart and ingenuous simplicity were

A parallel to the beatitudes from an Essene hymnbook.

the essential religious virtues. Jesus and the Essenes thought that the social outcasts and oppressed would become the first in the very near divine future: "for theirs is the kingdom of heaven," and "those who mourn will be comforted." Jesus certainly did not mean us to give a sentimental slant to these sayings, as the immediately following "woes," addressed to the "rich," the "satiated," and "those who laugh," prove. These people will have to sorrow and weep when the kingdom comes. Now for the first time, by using the new texts from the Dead Sea, we can understand the phrase "the poor in spirit," for this was a title of honor among the Essenes.[114] These were the poor to whom the Holy Spirit is given. In one passage of the Essene hymn book (18:14–15) the author thanks God for having appointed him preacher of his grace; he is "to preach to the humble the abundant mercy of God, and salvation from his eternal fountain, and to declare eternal joy to the oppressed in spirit and to them that mourn." These correspond to "the meek," "the poor in spirit," and "those who mourn" of the first three beatitudes of Jesus.

An even more significant parallel to Jesus' beatitudes and "woes" occurs in Jewish writings that are not Essene, it is true, but which belong to the fringe of the Essene cult.[115] These are the so-called *Testaments of the Patriarchs* which we possess in a Christian recension. It is easy, however, to detect the Jewish

77

provenance of these writings. The work is presented in the form
of the valedictory speeches of the twelve sons of Jacob. Judah
speaks about salvation at the end of time: "And there will be
one people of God and one language; and the deceitful spirit of
Belial will be no more, for he will be consumed in the eternal
fire. Those who died in sorrow will rise again in joy, the poor[116]
will become rich, the hungry will be filled, the weak will be
made strong, and those who died for the Lord's sake will awake
to life. The heart of Jacob will run with exultation, and the
eagles of Israel will swoop with joy; but the godless will mourn,
and sinners weep, and all the nations will praise the Lord for all
eternity."

The similarity between the beatitudes and "woes" of Jesus, and
the *Testament of Judah* is obvious. The Jewish author has
poetically expanded the common tradition and elaborated it in
respect of the resurrection of the dead. He says that those who
have died for the Lord's sake will awake to life, whereas Jesus
promises that the persecuted will inherit the kingdom of
heaven. This shows that the *Testaments of the Patriarchs* are
a half Essene work. It is true that genuine Essenes believed in
paradise, and hell, and in eternal life; but they did not believe,
as did the Pharisees and, later, the Christians, in the resurrection
of the dead. It is very strange that in the first three gospels, Jesus
too speaks about eternal life, but never explicitly of the resurrection of the dead—with the exception of his conversation with
the Sadducees "who say there is no resurrection" (Mk. 12:18–
27),[117] and when, in apparently secondary passages, he is speaking about his own resurrection. Is this accidental?

After what has been said about the Essenes, we require to explain how it is that the profoundly human beatitudes of Jesus
breathe the spirit of those Essenes who, although less un-
friendly in his times, still had not discarded their misanthropic
theology of hate. It must be noted in this connection, that radical
sects can often be quite amiable, and the Essene writings are
distinguished by their fervent piety. Both the Jewish classical
historian Josephus, and the philosopher Philo of Alexandria are

"Rejoice, you living ones!" A Greek inscription from a Jewish grave, beginning of the first century B.C. The deceased was, presumably, a Sadducee.

not far wrong when they depict the Essenes as men like Tolstoy. In the course of time, an inhuman ideology can produce almost human consequences. This happened with the Essenes. This humanization was fully worked out in Jewish circles that existed on the fringes of Essenism and were simultaneously influenced by the sensitivity of classical Judaism. Jesus was familiar with the ideas current in these circles, and incorporated them into his transvaluation of all values.

The Essenes believed that their final victory and the annihilation of evil were predestined by God. If the end has not yet come, one has to be subject to the evil powers of this world. Hence the way one lives in these times is regulated as follows: "Show eternal, secret hatred to the men of destruction, leaving to them property and the produce of labor, as a slave shows humility to him who rules over him. But at the same time let everyone be mindful of the predestined time—the day of vengeance."[118] This view gave rise to a kind of inhuman humanity, so that the Essenes could say of themselves: "I will repay no one with evil; I will visit men with good, for God judges all things that live and he will repay . . . I will not give up the struggle with the men of destruction until the day of vengeance, and I will not turn away my anger from wicked men and will not

79

rest until God appoints judgment."[119]

The Essene discovery that evil can be overcome with good has proved a mighty weapon in the history of the world. As we shall see, this idea was developed further by Jesus, and taken over by Christianity—even independently of Jesus' doctrine of love.[120] The rule: "Do not resist one who is evil" (Mt. 5:39), penetrated right down to modern times, and reached Gandhi, who learned of it through Christianity, and grafted it onto ancient Indian ideas. This originally Essene idea thus helped to liberate India by passive resistance.

History has shown that an enemy can be overcome by goodness, even if one does not love him, and even if he becomes no better as a result of the good that is done to him. This was what the Essenes wanted; but it is hard to fulfill these two conditions. It is only human nature to begin to love the one to whom one does good, and more important, when we do real good to someone—possible only if we love him a little—as a rule, that person is made better. Those groups who lived on the fringe of Essenism outgrew the Essene theology of hate, and hence affirmed these very consequences of doing good to one's enemy. In the *Testaments of the Patriarchs* already mentioned, especially in *The Testament of Benjamin,* the loving conquest of the sinner becomes an important moral imperative. "The good man has no darkness in his looks, for he has compassion upon all, even upon sinners when they plot evil against him. Thus he who does good overcomes the wicked for he is protected by goodness . . . My children, if your hearts are true, even wicked men will be at peace with you, and the avaricious will not only refrain from passion, but restore what they have taken from the oppressed . . . A true heart does not have two tongues—one to bless with and another to curse, one to scold and another to praise, one for sorrow and another for joy, one for peace and another for turmoil, one for flattery and another for truth, one for poverty and another for wealth—but preserves one and the same serenity towards all. It is not two-faced and double-eared . . . but all the works of Belial are devious and possess no simplicity."[121]

The same spirit was expressed by Jesus when he said: "You have heard that it was said, 'An eye for an eye and a tooth for a tooth' (Ex. 21:24–25).[122] But I say to you, Do not resist one who is evil. But if any one strikes you on the right cheek, turn to him the other also; and if any one would sue you and take your coat, let him have your cloak as well; and if any one forces you to go one mile, go with him two miles. Give to him who begs from you, and do not refuse him who would borrow from you.[123] You have heard that it was said, 'You shall love your neighbor[124] (Lev. 19:18) and hate your enemy.' But I say to you, Love your enemies and pray for those who persecute you, so that you may be sons of your Father who is in heaven; for he makes his sun rise on the evil and on the good, and sends rain on the just and on the unjust . . . You, therefore, must be perfect, as your heavenly Father is perfect" (Mt. 5:38–48).

According to *The Testament of Benjamin,* one must not have "two tongues—one to bless with and another to curse . . . but all the works of Belial are devious and possess no simplicity." According to Jesus, in loving one's neighbor one must be undivided as God is undivided. Even in the Old Testament the saying "an eye for an eye" was not taken literally. Jesus wanted to take the interpretation of this biblical saying from Exodus further by explaining "stripe for stripe" as meaning turning the other cheek to receive yet another stroke. This, too, was in harmony with the pietistic spirit of the Essene fringe. According to *The Testaments of the Patriarchs,*[125] the leading patriarch Zebulun went so far as surreptitiously to take a garment out to a poor man he saw shivering in the winter's cold. On one occasion, being able to find nothing to give to a poor man, he accompanied him seven stages of his journey, wailing all the time, for his heart went out in sympathy to the man.

It was from the Essene fringe, too, that Jesus took over both the idea that one ought not to resist one who is evil and the idea of good news addressed particularly to the poor and outcast. The doctrine of the Essene fringe about maintaining the same relationship to all men without distinction was developed by Jesus to become the command to love one's enemies and to love sinners specially. When the Pharisees upbraided him for eating in the company of publicans and sinners, he replied: "Those who are well have no need of a physician, but those who are sick"; and he added at once: "I came not to call the righteous, but sinners" (Mk. 2:16–17).

The paradox of Jesus' break with customary biblical morality was marvelously expressed in the parable of the workers in the vineyard (Mt. 20:1–16). A proprietor went out to hire workers for his vineyard, and promised each one a daily wage of one denarius. In the evening he paid them all the same wage irrespective of the length of time they had worked. Those who had started work early began to complain, and so the proprietor said to one of them: " 'Friend, I am doing you no wrong; did you not agree with me for a denarius? Take what belongs to you, and go; I choose to give to this last as I give to you. Am I not allowed to do what I choose with what belongs to me? Or do you begrudge my generosity?' So the last will be first, and the first last."

Here as elsewhere the principle of reward is accepted by Jesus, but all the norms of the usual concepts of the righteousness of God are abrogated. One might think that this comes about because, in his all-embracing love and mercy, God makes no distinctions between men; but with Jesus, the transvaluation of all values is not idyllic: even misfortune does not distinguish between the sinner and the just man. On one occasion someone brought the news to Jesus about the Galileans whose blood Pilate mixed with their sacrifices. The bystanders obviously expected a political reply, but Jesus said: "Do you think that these Galileans were worse sinners than all the other Galileans, because they suffered thus? I tell you, No; but unless you repent you will all likewise perish. Or those eighteen upon whom the tower in Siloam fell and killed them, do you think that they were worse offenders than all the others who dwelt in Jerusalem? I tell you, No; but unless you repent you will all likewise perish" (Lk. 13:1–5).

Lily on a Jewish coin.

We might say, therefore, that Jesus' concept of the righteousness of God is incommensurabe to reason: man cannot measure it, but can grasp and understand it. It leads to the preaching of the kingdom in which the last will be first, and the first last. It leads also from the Sermon on the Mount to Golgotha where the just man is to die the death of a criminal. It is at once profoundly moral and yet beyond good and evil. In this demonic view, all the "important," customary virtues and the well-knit personality, worldly dignity and the proud insistence upon the formal fulfillment of the law, are fragmentary and empty. Socrates questioned the intellectual side of the person; Jesus questioned the moral aspect of the person. Is this accidental?

THE KINGDOM

One day they sent spies to watch Jesus and to catch him out in what he said. " 'Teacher,' they said to him, 'we know that you speak and teach rightly, and show no partiality. Is it lawful for us to give tribute to Caesar, or not?' But he perceived their craftiness, and said to them, 'Show me a coin. Whose likeness and inscription has it?' They said, 'Caesar's.' He said to them, 'Then render to Caesar the things that are Caesar's, and to God the things that are God's' " (cf. Lk. 20:20–26).

Once again Jesus had succeeded in evading capture, while at the same time making his meaning unmistakably clear. One cannot serve two masters, God and mammon. Money comes from Caesar, and so it must be handed over to him. Quite certainly the saying did not express friendship with the Romans, but it showed also that Jesus was no supporter of revolt against the Romans. His ethical teaching made that impossible. He was well aware of social reality; but that was not the most important thing. Once you have allowed yourself to enter the game, however, you must play according to the rules. "Make friends quickly with your accuser, while you are going with him to court, lest your accuser hand you over to the judge, and the judge to the guard, and you be put in prison; truly I say to you, you will never get out till you have paid the last penny" (Mt. 5:25–26).

It is hard to concur with those who affirm[126] that Jesus was executed by Pilate, not without some reason, as a political agitator, or even that he was the leader of a gang in the Jewish war of liberation against Rome. In addition to the trial of Jesus, the chief evidence cited in support of this affirmation is that Jesus had preached the kingdom of heaven. "Heaven" is a circumlocution for "God" and people in general believed that when the kingdom of God came, Israel would be freed from the yoke of Rome. At that time most Jews hated the Roman army of occu-

A Roman denarius. Front: image of Tiberius Caesar.
Back: the goddess of peace.

pation, and the party known as the Zealots[127] saw the battle
against Rome as divinely willed; and Jewish Zealot terrorists
made the country unsafe. One of the twelve apostles had certainly been a Zealot at one time.[128]

The fundamental teaching of the Zealots "was the demand for
the sole rule of God, which led to a radical breach with the
Roman Caesar's claims to sovereignty; it was linked with the
expectation that, through battle with the Roman oppressor, the
eschatological liberation of Israel at the end of time would be
ushered in."[129] Although it is possible that the Zealots, too,
spoke about the kingdom of heaven, at that time the phrase had
in fact become an anti-Zealot slogan. Because there are clear
similarities between the rabbinic idea of the kingdom and that of
Jesus, we may assume that Jesus took up and developed their
idea. This idea did not appear among the Essenes.

Among the Jews, the kingdom or rule of God meant that the
one and only God rules *de jure,* even today; but only in the
eschatological future will "the kingdom of God be revealed upon
all the inhabitants of the world"[130] *de facto.* If Israel now lan-
guishes under a foreign yoke, at the end God alone will rule in
Sion. The anti-Zealot groups, too, cherished this hope, and the

85

Stamped seal of the tenth Roman legion, from Jerusalem.

disciples of Jesus thought likewise. According to Acts 1:6–8 they asked the risen Lord: "Lord, will you at this time restore the kingdom to Israel?" In the Book of Revelation we hear jubilation at the fall of Rome, but the "historical Jesus" of the gospels is silent on this point. Could the friend of the poor and the persecuted be an enemy of Romans? All the same we can understand that, even if Jesus had foreseen the fall of Rome, the evangelists might not have mentioned it, so as not to cast even more suspicion upon the founder of their religion.

The domination of Israel by a foreign power was seen as a punishment for her sins. "If the house of Israel transgresses the law, foreign nations will rule over her, and if they keep the law, mourning, tribulation and lamentation will depart from her."[131] In other words, "If Israel kept the words of the law given to them, no people or kingdom would rule over them." And what does the law say? "Take upon you the yoke of my name and emulate one another in the fear of God and practise kindness to one another."[132] Thus, even today, there may be individuals who are, so to speak, citizens of the kingdom of heaven. "Every-

Shekel (front). From the period of the Jewish war against the Romans, 66–70 A.D.
Shekel (back).

one who takes the yoke of the law upon him will have taken off his shoulders the yoke of government and of daily sorrows. But whoever puts off the yoke of the law will be burdened with the yoke of government and of daily sorrows."[133]

Israel must want to do only the will of God, then the kingdom of heaven will be revealed to them. "If Israel at the Red Sea had said, 'He is king for all eternity,' no nation or language would have ruled over them; but they said (Ex. 15:18), 'the Lord will reign for ever and ever.' "[134] This saying was apparently directed against not only the futuristic hopes of the apocalyptists, but the Zealots who wanted to take heaven by force. When the Zealots had forcibly assumed government and the rebellion had been bloodily suppressed by Rome, one of the scribes complained of "the rulers of the city of Judah, who have put off the yoke of heaven and assumed the yoke of the government of flesh and blood."[135] This view was shared by Rabbi Jochanan ben Sakkai.[136] After the destruction of Jerusalem, when he saw the daughter of Nicodemus assuaging her hunger with grains of barley picked from the dung of an Arab horse, he wept and said: "Blessed are you O Israel! If you do the will of God no nation and no language shall rule over you. But if you do not the will of God you will be delivered into the hands of an inferior race."[137]

According to rabbinic literature, the yoke of foreign domination would be removed from Israel by the appearance of the kingdom of heaven. The apocalyptists[138] believed that then Satan and his powers would also be destroyed, and so thought Jesus. In other respects, as we have said, Jesus' concept of the kingdom of heaven is related to that of the rabbis. According to Jesus, too, the coming of the rule of God, and hope in the eschatological savior are two different aspects of the expectation of the end, and the idea of the kingdom of God and of the Son of man were never confused in his mind.[139] According to both Jesus and the rabbis, the kingdom of heaven emerges, indeed, out of the power of God, but is realized upon earth by men, and there are already individuals who live in the kingdom of God. Man, then, can and should work for the realization of the kingdom: "Repent, for the kingdom of heaven is at hand" (Mt. 4:17).

The first to point out from the preaching of the kingdom of God, the eschatological orientation of the message of Jesus was Hermann Samuel Reimarus (1694–1768). Lessing, as we know, then published fragments of his writings. Starting from Lessing's text, Albert Schweitzer then elaborated his "logical eschatology": "To be worthy of consideration, Jesus' mode of thought must be either completely eschatological or completely non-eschatological."[140] Reimarus certainly would not have agreed with this. In the final version of his work—still in manuscript[141]—he distinguishes between Jesus' non-eschatological moral preaching of repentance and "his main purpose, which was to inaugurate a kingdom."[142] Modern portrayals of Jesus, however, trace his eschatology along a different line. The warning of the great Christian and religious socialist, Leonard Ragaz, was in vain: "The notion is quite untenable, that Jesus built a kind of ethic and theology upon his expectation of the imminence of the kingdom of God. This sort of thing may well happen in the study of a theologian or a philosopher . . . The relationship is

Hermann Samuel Reimarus.

Albert Schweitzer.

quite the reverse from what the eschatological systematizers imagine. It is not the eschatological expectation which determines Jesus' understanding of God and of man . . . , but, conversely, his understanding of God and of man which determines his eschatological expectation . . . To fail t see this one must have already put on a professor's spectacles."[143]

Schweitzer was still concerned with the painful truth, but the later eschatologists fell into a non-committal admiration of an alleged pan-eschatologism of Jesus. If we understand every saying of Jesus in a purely eschatological sense, so that eschatology becomes consciously interpreted as existential, then we arrive at the conclusion that the demands of Jesus are not morally binding. One New Testament scholar has said that turning the other cheek is only allowed because it is a "messianic license"—otherwise this sort of thing would be revolutionary. This is a correct assessment, for the preaching of Jesus is indeed revolutionary, subversive.

89

For Jesus as for the rabbis, the kingdom of God is both present and future, but the perspectives are different. When Jesus was asked when the kingdom was to come he said: "The kingdom of God is not coming with signs to be observed; nor will they say, 'Lo, here it is!' or 'There!' for behold, the kingdom of God is in the midst of you" (Lk. 17:21–21). He said: "But if it is by the finger of God that I cast out demons, then the kingdom of God has come upon you" (Lk. 11:20). There are individuals, therefore, who are already in the kingdom of heaven, not, as with the rabbis, because it was always so, but because at a specific point in time the kingdom has broken out upon earth. "From the days of John the Baptist until now the kingdom of heaven has suffered violence, and men of violence take it by force" (Mt. 11:12).

That, then, is the "realized eschatology" of Jesus.[144] He is the only Jew of ancient times known to us, who preached not only that men were on the threshold of the end of time, but that the new age of salvation had already begun.[145] This new age had begun with John the Baptist. He made the great break-through, but was not himself a member of the kingdom. The eruption of the kingdom of God meant also its expansion among men. "The kingdom of heaven is like leaven which a woman took and hid in three measures of meal, till all was leavened" (Mt. 13:33). On the growth of the kingdom of heaven Jesus also said: "It is like a grain of mustard seed which a man took and sowed in his garden; and it grew and became a tree, and the birds of the air made nests in its branches" (Lk. 13:18–19).

A similar image is to be found in the Essene hymnbook.[146] The poet compares the congregation to a tree, "around whose luxuriant foliage all the beasts of the field graze . . . and its branches shelter all the birds. But all of the weeds rise above it." This is a symbol of the wicked world all around. Even the tree of life is concealed—"the seal of its mystery remains unobserved, unrecognized." God himself guards its secret—the outsider "sees but does not recognize, and thinks, but does not believe in the source of life." This reminds us of the words of Jesus: "To you it has been given to know the secrets of the kingdom of heaven, but to them it has not been given" (Mt. 13:11–15). What is much more important is that the parable of the grain of mustard seed resembles the Essene symbol for the community. Thus, for Jesus, the kingdom of heaven is not only the eschatological rule of God that has dawned already, but a divinely willed movement that spreads among men over the earth. It is not only—as with the Jews—the kingship, but the kingdom of God: a realm that extends to embrace ever more people, into which a man may enter and find his inheritance, in which there are the great and the small. That is why Jesus called the twelve to be *fishers of men*[147] and to heal and to preach everywhere: "The kingdom of heaven is at hand" (Mt. 10:5–16). For this reason he demanded of some that they should leave all behind them and follow him. We do not mean to assert that Jesus wanted to found a church or even a simple community, but that he wanted to start a movement. Stated in exaggeratedly ecclesiological terms, we might say: the eruption of the kingdom of heaven is a process in which ultimately the invisible Church becomes identical with the visible.

In the message of the kingdom is fulfilled that which Jesus recognized and desired. There the unconditional love of God for all becomes visible, and the boundaries between sinner and just person are shattered. Human dignity becomes null and void, the last become first, and the first become last. The poor, the hungry, the meek, the mourners, and the persecuted inherit the kingdom of heaven. In Jesus' message of the kingdom, the social factor does not, however, seem to be the decisive thing. His revolution has to do chiefly with the transvaluation of all the usual moral values, and hence his promise is specially for sinners: "Truly, I say to you, the tax collectors and the harlots go into the kingdom of God before you" (Mt. 21:31–32). Jesus appealed to the social outcasts and the despised, and the same had been true also of John the Baptist—to judge by his words.

Even the non-eschatological ethical teaching of Jesus can presumably be oriented towards his message of the kingdom.[148]

Because Satan and his powers will be overthrown and the present world-order shattered, they are to be regarded as almost indifferent, and ought not to be strengthened by opposition. Therefore, one ought not to resist evil; therefore, one ought to love one's enemy and not provoke the Roman empire to attack. For when the kingdom of God appears, all this will vanish.

Jesus and the woman with the hemorrhage. From a Roman catacomb, end of the third century.

THE SON

Jesus is portrayed in the gospels as a miracle-worker. Rabbinic literature tells us of four such men, who operated before the destruction of the second temple. Two[149] of these were Galileans, and of them we are told, in passing, that they were very poor men. One of these two was the laborer Abba Hilkia.[150] On one occasion when two scribes[151] had been sent to ask him to pray for rain, he behaved very strangely towards them. The reason for this, in part, was undoubtedly the tension which existed between miracle-workers and the scribes. The second Galilean, Rabbi Hanina bar Dossa, lived a generation after Jesus and was famous for his miracles of healing. A heavenly voice said of him: "The whole world will be nourished because of my son Hanina —and a morsel of John's bread will satisfy my son Hanina for a week."[152]

It is no accident that the heavenly voice addressed Hanina as "My son." The miracle-worker is closer to God than other men. When Hanina had healed the son of Rabbi Jochanan ben Sakkai by prayer,[153] the scribe's wife said, "Is Hanina greater, then, than you?" and he answered, "No, but he is like a slave before a king, and I am like a higher official before a king."

Something similar is said about Honi the "drawer of circles"[154] who died in the spring of 65 B.C. Once, when he was asked to pray for rain, he drew a circle round himself and prayed: "Ruler of the world, your children have turned to me, because I am in your presence like one of your household. I swear by your great name that I will not move from this place until you have pity upon your children." Then, when rain came, the chief of the Pharisees at that time, Simeon ben Shatah, complained of his audacious behavior: "Were you not Honi I would excommunicate you. What am I to do with you? You ingratiate yourself with God and he does what you ask, as when a son curries favor with his father, who then does what the son wants.

If he says: 'Father, let me bathe in warm water or in cold, give me nuts, almonds, apricots or pomegranates,' he grants his request." The miracle-worker is close to God—like a household companion, like a son.

Honi was killed in the civil war between the two Maccabean brothers, Aristobolos and Hyrkanos. Josephus[155] recounts how he went into hiding on account of the war, but was fetched to the camp of Hyrkanos to curse Aristobolos who occupied the city of Jerusalem. Refusing to have anything to do with such a thing, he was executed. A medieval Hebrew author[156] was perceptive enough to detect that Josephus had misunderstood and expanded the oral tradition concerning Honi's death; so, in his redaction of the story, he left out the alleged reason for Honi's concealment. Honi hid not from fear of the war, but because such was the habit of this pious miracle-worker; he was a hidden just man like Hanan "the hidden" of a later date. "When rain was needed the scribes used to send school children to Hanan to touch the hem of his cloak and say: 'Abba, Abba,[157] give us rain!' Then he would address God: 'Ruler of the world, do this for the sake of those who cannot distinguish between a Father (Abba) who can give rain and a Father who cannot.' And why did they call him Hanan the Hidden? Because he used to hide himself."[158]

We see, then, that in those days there was an understandable tension between the miracle-working charismatics and the class of scribes. Nor is it strange that such holy men should practise poverty by compulsion or freely; it was in character for these people to perform their miracles in secret. Humanly speaking, all of this applies to Jesus. Thus, for example, Jesus commanded the person who had been cured to say nothing about his cure; and this, apparently, was one of the reasons why he did not want to reveal completely the secret of his divine election.

We have seen how the relationship to God of three of the miracle-workers belonging to the period of the second temple was described as that of a son to his father. The earliest, Honi, prayed to God as a member of his household, and was likened to a son who was accustomed to ingratiate himself with his

The sacrifice of Isaac. Mosaic from the synagogue of Beth Alpha, first century.

father. Hanina stood before God as his personal servant, and was addressed by a heavenly voice as "my son!" Hanan the Hidden took up the children's word "Father," and in prayer described God as "the Father who can give rain." Could it have been otherwise than that such men, who were like sons to God, should have addressed God as "Father"? Jesus certainly spoke in this way.[159]

If Jesus was like a son to God, this denoted more than the mere closeness of the miracle-worker. For him, sonship was also the consequence of his election through the heavenly voice at his baptism. As son he knew his Father in heaven. "I thank thee, Father, Lord of heaven and earth, that thou hast hidden these things from the wise and understanding and revealed them to babes; yea, Father, for such things have been delivered to me by my Father; and no one knows the Son[160] except the Father, and no one knows the Father except the Son and any one to whom the Son chooses to reveal him" (Mt. 11:25–27).[161]

95

Not until the discovery of the Essene writings at the Dead Sea did we know about any such high degree of self-consciousness in ancient Judaism. Now we know: the exultant cry of Jesus is in line with Essene hymn writing.[162] Jesus' hymn begins with the same word as do most of the prayers in the hymnbook, and even the rhythmic structure is similar. The Essene author, like Jesus, says that "the simple will become wise."[163] As for Jesus, this wisdom consists in knowledge of the mysteries of God. "Through me you have enlightened the mind of many and shown strength countless times, for you have revealed your wonderful mysteries to me and confirmed my status by the secret of your miracles, and for the sake of your glory you have acted marvelously in the sight of many, so as to declare your mighty deeds to all who live" (Hymnbook 4:27–29). This is the mentality of the charismatic apocalyptist who has access to the mysteries of God, through which he is able to "enlighten the minds of many."

According to the gospels, Jesus was addressed by the heavenly voice as "Son" as early as his baptism; but the presumption is justified that at that time he was simply being described as the chosen servant. Not until the voice at the Transfiguration was he truly named "Son." Jesus took Peter, and John, and James, and climbed with them up to a mountain; his face became different, and his clothes became shining white; Moses and Elijah spoke to him. When they departed, Jesus said to Peter: "Rabbi, it is good for us to be here; let us make three huts, one for you, one for Moses, and one for Elijah." Then a cloud came and overshadowed them and a voice out of the cloud said: "This is my only[164] Son, hear him." Jesus was there alone (Lk. 9:28–36).

Even E. Meyer[165] regarded this vision as authentic. The heavenly voice is significant. The words "hear him" are made intelligible by the prophecy of Moses: "The Lord your God will raise up for you a prophet like me from among you, from your brethren—him you shall heed" (Dt. 18:15). The fact that there appeared two great prophets of old, Moses and Elijah, under-

Grape harvest. From a mosaic near Beth Shean, fifth century A.D.

lined the meaning of the voice: Jesus is the prophetic preacher
to whom the Old Testament had pointed. The voice designated
Jesus "only Son," as God had said to Abraham: "Take your son,
your only son Isaac, whom you love, . . . and offer him there as
a burnt offering . . ." (Gen. 22:2) This alludes to the coming
martyrdom of Jesus. Luke (9:31) says, in fact, that on the
occasion of the Transfiguration, Moses and Elijah spoke with
Jesus about his imminent departure in Jerusalem.

Jesus linked together his sense of sonship, his predestination
as prophetic preacher, and his knowledge of his tragic end, in
the parable of the tenants of the vineyard (cf. Lk. 20:9–19).
This was narrated in the temple in the presence of the high
priests before Jesus' death. "The master of the vineyard sent
a servant to the tenants of the vineyard to collect his dues. The
tenants beat him and sent him back. Again he sent another
servant whom they beat and mocked. He sent yet another whom
they wounded and threw out. At last he sent his son, thinking
that they would respect him. But when the tenants of the vineyard saw him they said to one another: 'This is the heir, let us
kill him and the inheritance will be ours.' They took him out of
the vineyard and killed him. What will the master of the vineyard do to them? He will come and destroy these tenants and
give the vineyard to others." They thought how they might
apprehend him, but they feared the crowd, observing that the
parable was aimed at themselves.

97

Here we are right at the center of Jesus' clash with the Sadducees, the temple aristocracy—the clash that was to lead to his death. The high priests interpreted the parable correctly: *they* were the wicked tenants of the vineyard who on account of their office held a monopoly over the people of God—for the vineyard is the people of Israel;[166] but they will be destroyed, and God will give his vineyard to others. This did indeed happen after the destruction of the temple, when this priestly caste was destroyed, and it disappeared for good. The servants who had been sent to the vineyard were God's prophetic messengers who had been persecuted and slain. Counted in their number was Jesus, the Son. There is a Jewish parable[167] of a proprietor and his wicked, thieving tenants. The proprietor took the estate away from them and gave it to their sons; but these were even worse than their fathers. Then a son was born to the proprietor. He drove out the tenants, and put his son into the estate. Jesus apparently knew a similar parable, but he adapted it to become a tragedy: in his version the son is killed.

Jesus' sonship leads then, not to life, but to the death that many prophets before him had suffered. After the Transfiguration, his awareness of the sonship of God was linked with the premonition that he had to die. Even before his entry into Jerusalem he sensed his tragic end; but for Jesus this knowledge of divine sonship was scarcely identical with his consciousness of being the Messiah. The Jews of those days were, it is true, acquainted with the image of martyrdom as an atoning sacrifice; but it is a refreshing result of philological exactitude to be able, by cold analysis of the text, to establish that Jesus did not intend to die in order to expiate the sins of others by his own brief passion. Nor did he see himself as the suffering, atoning servant of God of the prophet Isaiah. This idea arose retrospectively in the early Church—not until after the crucifixion.[168] Jesus had neither subtly nor mythically worked out the idea of his own death from the ancient writings, and then carried out the idea.[169] He was no "Christ of the festival," for he wrestled with death to the very end.

THE SON OF MAN

"Then Jesus and his disciples traveled to the villages around Caesarea Philippi. There he asked them: 'Whom do men say that I am?' And they replied: 'John the Baptist, others say, Elijah, and others again say, one of the prophets.' Then he said to them: 'But whom do you say that I am?' Peter said: 'The Messiah.' Then he dared them to speak about him to anyone" (cf. Mk. 8:7–30). According to Matthew (16:17–19) on this occasion he said to Peter: "Blessed are you, Simon Bar Jona! For flesh and blood has not revealed this to you, but my Father who is in heaven."[170]

According to this report, the people, too, regarded Jesus as a prophet. The people identified John the Baptist with Elijah who had returned, and this belief in the return of Elijah was but a special form of hope in the renewal of prophecy by a prophet at the end of time.[171] Jesus, too, had seen himself as a prophet, and said that he was going up to Jerusalem, "for it cannot be that a prophet should perish away from Jerusalem" (Lk. 13:33). Elsewhere throughout the New Testament we find clear traces of this view; and the Jewish Christian sects of Ebionites and Nazarenes concurred in stressing the prophetic dignity of Jesus.[172] The accounts of the gospels seem to contradict the view that Jesus regarded himself as the eschatological prophet *par excellence.*

Matthew's version of Jesus' words to Peter have an authentic ring about them. Can one, then, following the belief of the Church, think that Jesus regarded himself as the Messiah, or must one agree with those who affirm, that Jesus' life was "non-Messianic"?[173] The latter affirmation rests upon the fact that Jesus himself apparently never used the word "Messiah," and always spoke of the Son of man in the third person, as though he himself were not identical with that person. The gospel sayings about the Son of man fall into three groups: those referring to the coming Son of man, those referring to his suffering and resurrection, and those in which the Son of man seems to be at work in the present. "Foxes have holes, and birds of the air have nests; but the Son of man[174] has nowhere to lay his head" (Mt. 8:19–20). In this and other sayings the Aramaic or Hebrew term "Son of man" means simply "man." This group of sayings, therefore, has nothing to do with Jesus' eschatological hope. The second group is certainly a product of early Christianity. The Jews were unacquainted with the notion of a suffering and resurrected "Son of man." The only sayings relevant to Jesus' doctrine of the Redeemer are, therefore, those that speak of the coming Son of man.

The Son of man appears in the Old Testament in the Book of Daniel. There (7:9–14) in a vision, Daniel describes the coming judgment of God upon all the kingdoms of the world: "As I looked, thrones were placed and one that was ancient of days took his seat; . . . the court sat in judgment, and the books were opened . . . I saw in the night visions, and behold, with clouds of heaven there came one like a son of man, and he came to the Ancient of Days and was presented before him. And to him was given dominion and glory and kingdom, and all peoples, nations, and languages should serve him; his dominion is an everlasting dominion, which shall not pass away, and his kingdom one that shall not be destroyed."

For Daniel, the Son of man is a symbol of the "saints of the Most High"; but, as we learn from other scriptures, notably the *Ethiopian Book of Enoch,* this identification is secondary. Originally the Son of man was the man-like eschatological judge. Jesus spoke of him: "When the Son of man comes in his glory, and all the angels with him, then he will sit on his glorious throne. Before him will be gathered all the nations, and he will separate them one from another as a shepherd separates the sheep from the goats, and he will place the sheep at his right hand, but the goats at the left. Then the King will say to those at his right hand, 'Come, O blessed of my Father, inherit the kingdom prepared for you from the foundation of the

The Son of man.
From the Ghent
altar by the broth-
ers Hubert and
Jan van Eyck. St.
Bavo's, Ghent.

world; . . .' Then he will say to those at his left hand, 'Depart from me, you cursed, into the eternal fire prepared for the devil and his angels; . . .' And they will go away into eternal punishment, but the righteous into eternal life" (Mt. 25:31–36).

In all of the sources the figure of this one like a man is always portrayed with the same economy of line. The Son of man has a superhuman, heavenly sublimity. He is the cosmic judge at the end of time; seated upon the throne of God, he will judge the whole human race with the aid of the heavenly hosts, consigning the just to blessedness and sinners to the pit of hell; and he will execute the sentence he passes. Frequently he is identified[175] with the Messiah, but he can also be identified with Enoch of the bible, who was taken up into heaven.[176] According to the *Testament of Abraham*[177] the Son of man—Ben Adam in Hebrew—is literally Adam's son Abel, who was killed by the wicked Cain, for God desired that every man be judged by a man. At the second judgment the twelve tribes of Israel will judge the whole of creation; not until the third judgment will God himself judge. This apocalyptic tradition explains why Jesus said to the twelve: "You, who have persevered with me in my tribulations, when the Son of man sits upon his glorious throne will also sit upon thrones, judging the twelve tribes of Israel" (cf. Mt. 19:28; Lk. 22:28–30).

In one of the Essene fragments[178] Melchizedek the Old Testament priest-king of Jerusalem in the time of Abraham figures as the prophet at the end of time. In company with the angels, from on high he will judge men and the wicked spirits of Belial. It is of him the psalmist speaks: "God has taken his place in the divine council; in the midst of the gods he holds judgment" (Ps. 82:1). Elsewhere, too, Jewish tradition understands the word "god" in biblical texts as simply "judge," but the Essene identification at the same time proves what majesty could be attributed to the "manlike" judge at the end of time.

The view that the executor of the last judgment would be the biblical Melchizedek was based upon Psalm 110: "The Lord says to my lord: 'Sit at my right hand, . . . You are a priest for ever after the order of Melchizedek . . .' " The Hebrew phrase "after the order of" could be understood in the sense that in this psalm God is addressing Melchizedek himself. Thus it was understood by the Essene author. According to the usual interpretation, he who will sit at God's right hand is not Melchizedek himself, but merely one who is the same kind of person as Melchizedek. That is how Jesus understood this psalm. On one occasion, reported in Mk. 12:35–37, he quoted the beginning of Psalm 110 with reference to the Messiah. The second time, before being handed over to the Romans, he alluded to the words of this psalm when the high priest asked him if he were the Messiah. He said: "But from now on the Son of man shall be seated at the right hand of the power of God" (Lk. 22:69). Those present correctly understood this as Jesus' indirect admission of his Messianic dignity.

It is quite certain that in his own lifetime Jesus became accepted by many—not just by Peter—as the Messiah. Had it not been so, Pilate would not have written above the cross of Jesus: "King of the Jews."[179] On the other hand, the substance of many sayings makes it obvious that Jesus did not always refer to the coming Son of man in the third person simply because he wanted to preserve his incognito. At first he had been awaiting another; but in the end, the conviction gained strength that he himself was the coming Son of man. Otherwise the conversation at Caesarea Philippi, Jesus' words to Peter, and Jesus' answer to the high priest would not make sense. This saying in particular can hardly be an invention of the Church, for the evangelists have embroidered it, thinking that it was not a sufficiently unequivocal confession of his own Messiahship.[180]

The one like a man who sits upon the throne of God's glory, the sublime eschatological judge, is the highest conception of the Redeemer ever developed by ancient Judaism. Only one artist has captured it: Van Eyck. He depicted the Son of man, above the altar at Ghent, as a human being who is divine.[181] Could Jesus of Nazareth have understood himself thus? Let us not forget that he felt he was God's chosen one, his servant, the

Jerusalem.

only Son to whom the secrets of the heavenly Father were open. This very sense of sublime dignity could have led him in the end publicly to dare to identify himself with the Son of man; and in Judaism the Son of man was frequently understood as the Messiah.

The New Testament links Jesus' death with his Messiahship; but for Jesus himself, his premonition of death was scarcely connected with the notion of the Son of man. He who had commanded us not to resist evil, went to his death without a fight. At the end, had he realized that his execution was the crown of his transvaluation of all the usual values? By it the highest was indeed made lowest and the lowest highest: "For Christ also died for sins once for all, the righteous for the unrighteous, that he might bring us to God" (1 Pet. 3:18).

JERUSALEM

"At that very hour some Pharisees came, and said to him, 'Get away from here, for Herod wants to kill you.' And he said to them, 'Go and tell that fox, Behold, I cast out demons and perform cures today and tomorrow, and the third day I finish my course. Nevertheless I must go on my way today and tomorrow and the day following; for it cannot be that a prophet should perish away from Jerusalem'" (Lk. 13:31–33).

To Herod Antipas Jesus was the Baptist whom he had beheaded, risen from the dead, and he was set on taking his life. Jesus knew, then, that his life was in danger—a heavenly voice never comes out of a completely clear sky—but he did not want to die in Galilee where he preached the kingdom of heaven. He wanted to die in Jerusalem, reputed for "killing the prophets and stoning those who are sent to you" (Lk. 13:34). The ostensible reason for his pilgrimage was something else, however: the Passover was drawing near, and Jews were accustomed to making a pilgrimage to Jerusalem to sacrifice the paschal lamb and celebrate their deliverance from slavery in Egypt. Jesus, too, had longed earnestly to eat this paschal lamb with his disciples;[182] so his way of the cross began.

As Jesus approached the city he sent two disciples ahead to fetch an ass, and upon this he rode into Jerusalem. Entering the city, he was greeted with "Hosanna!" and a verse of a psalm (118:26), "Blessed be he who enters in the name of the Lord!" On pilgrimage festivals these words were sung and were used also to greet pilgrims as they arrived in Jerusalem.[183] Strewing garments[184] in his path may have been the people's way of showing honor to the prophet from Galilee (Mt. 21:11). He entered Jerusalem, visited the temple, and then went out to Bethany, a village on the outskirts of Jerusalem. There, among friends, he spent his last nights.[185] By day he went to Jerusalem and taught in the temple. The temple authorities asked him,

The Phasael tower in Jerusalem, built by Herod the Great.

indeed, by what authority he did this, but he replied, "Let me ask you a question: John's baptism, was it of God or of men?" This sent his interrogators into confusion. The Sadducean temple authorities had no love for the Baptist, so, they could not say that John's baptism was of God. However, to say that it was of men was too dangerous, for they feared the crowd who believed John the Baptist to have been a prophet of God. Therefore they merely said. "We do not know." Jesus said to them: "Nor do I tell you by whose authority I do this." There the matter rested (cf. Mk. 11:27–33).

This skirmish set off a series of clashes between Jesus and the temple hierarchy, in which he consciously took the initiative, and won over to himself the crowd who hated the Sadducean high priests. His prophetic anger was perfectly genuine; but what did he mean to accomplish: the victory of his cause, with the help of God and man—and without having to die—or the death of a prophet? According to the ancient report, Jesus' first encounter followed immediately upon the conversation concerning the baptism of John. In the parable of the tenants in the

The temple court. View towards the Golden Gate.

vineyard (Mk. 12:1–12) Jesus spoke of his death at the hands of the high priests, and proclaimed to them their own overthrow. "And they tried to arrest him, but feared the multitude, for they perceived that he had told the parable against them; . . ."

Thus he taught daily in the temple, and the high priests sought to destroy him; but they were afraid, for the crowd hung upon his words.[186] On one occasion, when some people said of the temple, "What stones, what a building!" he announced: "Do you see all that? Not one stone shall be left standing upon another that is not destroyed" (cf. Lk. 21:5–6). Forty years later, the temple went up in flames at the hands of the Romans. The unbearable Roman oppression provoked insurrection and terrorism by the fanatics, and the sanctuary in Jerusalem with a bulwark of the hated Sadducees who had made a pact with the Romans. Dislike sharpens vision, and many foresaw the destruction of the temple. Thus for example in 62 A.D. on the Feast of Tabernacles, it happened that Joshua the son of Ananias, a simple peasant, was seized by the Spirit in the temple, and suddenly poured forth a prophetic malediction in which he fore-

Herodian stones from the Wailing Wall of the temple in Jerusalem.

told the destruction of the temple. Like one possessed, he kept up his cry day and night in the streets of Jerusalem. The authorities dragged him before the Roman governor, Albinus, who had him scourged to the bone; but the man only went on repeating his gruesome prophecy. The governor then let him go free, considering him to be out of his mind.[187]

Jesus expressed his opposition to the abuses in the temple not only by words, but by deeds. As it often does at shrines, a brisk trade went on at the temple in Jerusalem in those days. Jesus was not the only one whose displeasure had been aroused by the tables of the money-changers, and the stalls of the dove-sellers at the place of sanctification;[188] but it was not until after Jesus' death that the scribes found practical measures to keep the trade necessary for the temple sacrifices out of the temple precincts. When Jesus visited the precincts of the temple, these measures were not yet effective. Having entered the temple, he began to drive out the traders, saying, "It is written,[189] 'My house shall

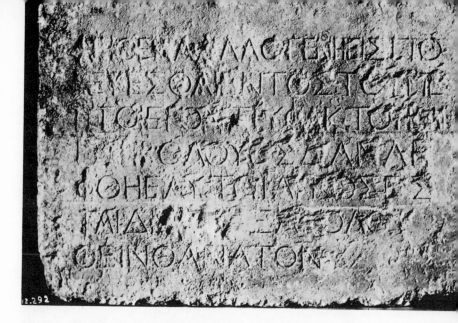

Greek inscription which announces that non-Jews are forbidden, on the pain of death, to enter the temple.

be called a house of prayer'; but you have made it a den of robbers"[190] (cf. Lk. 19:45–46).[191] St. John reports that Jesus also said: "I will destroy this temple that is made with hands, and in three days I will build another, not made with hands" (Mk. 14:58; cf. Mt. 26:61). In Mark (14:57–59), however, the saying is not genuine.[192]

It would seem that we do not have this saying in its original form: the three days are connected with the belief that Jesus rose on the third day. On the other hand, the saying really was expressed originally in the first person. Jesus spoke in the name of God[193] in the spirit of Jewish apocalyptism.[194] The present temple would be destroyed and another would then be raised up by the hand of God. The saying is, then, another prophecy about the destruction of the temple. As he was leaving Galilee, indeed, he said, "Behold, your house is forsaken" (Lk. 13:35). To announce this he was sent to Jerusalem, and, seen from this angle, his expulsion of the traders and the connected saying

Coin with vine leaf.

Judea Capta. Roman coin celebrating the victory of the Romans over the Jews.

The emperor Vespasian.

Coin of Bar Kochba with a picture of the temple, 122–135 A.D.

Relief on the Titus Arch in Rome. Triumphal procession with spoil from the temple in Jerusalem.

about the temple, was the climax of his prophetic mission to Jerusalem. This precipitated the catastrophe. The Sadducean priesthood, despised by everyone, found its one support in the temple; and this prophet from Galilee, publicly in the temple in front of the crowd assembled for the festival, had foretold not only the decline of this priestly caste, but the destruction of their temple. Moreover, making use of the bitter feeling there was about the trade that went on in the sanctuary, he actively struck a blow against the temple authorities. As we have seen, thirty years later, the authorities handed over Joshua ben Ananias to the Romans because he too prophesied the destruction of the temple. Throughout their whole empire, the Romans diligently protected all religious sanctuaries. They also made it their business to protect the high priests from agitators.

The ancient report[195] merely states that Jesus began to drive the traders out of the temple. Apparently he was not able to carry out his intention, and we do not know how many obeyed

The place where, according to tradition, the Last Supper took place.

Jewish Passover meal. From the Nuremberg Haggada.

his directions, nor have we any report of the reaction of the
crowd of pilgrims who were present. It is almost certain that
the temple guard eventually intervened. We may presume also
that the cleansing of the temple took place very shortly before
the arrest of Jesus which he had been able to avoid on the first
occasion. According to the first three gospels, which we follow
on this point, the Last Supper was a paschal meal. Jesus had,
therefore, already killed the paschal lamb. As it was prescribed
that the roasted lamb be eaten within the city, on the last evening
Jesus did not go back to Bethany, but remained in Jerusalem.[196]
We have no record of the host's name, for in those days pilgrims
were gladly received everywhere and anywhere. When night had
fallen he reclined at table with the twelve and said, " 'With all
my heart I have longed to eat this paschal lamb with you before

113

I die;[197] for I tell you: I will never eat it again until I eat it anew[198] in the kingdom of God.' And he took a cup of wine, recited the prayer of thanksgiving over it and said, 'Take it and share it among you; for I tell you, I will not again drink of the fruit of the vine until I drink it new in the kingdom of God.'[199] And he took bread, recited the thanksgiving over it and said, 'This is my body.' "[200]

Catastrophe seemed inevitable. Jesus made no secret to his disciples that he knew they would all be scattered[201] and not stay beside him, and he told Peter that before the cock crew he would deny him thrice[202]—and this really happened. As they were eating the feast, begun under the shadow of death, he said: "Behold the hand of him who betrays me is with me on the table" (Lk. 22:11). Had he discovered the betrayer? Earlier, probably after the clash in the temple, Judas Iscariot, one of the twelve, had gone to the high priests to deliver Jesus over to them, and they had promised to pay him (Mk. 14:10–11). We do not know why he did this, and the accounts of his death are contradictory. Most likely he disappeared after the betrayal, for there were plenty of people at that time who would have repaid him in blood for handing a Jew over to the Romans.

After the festival meal, the hymn of praise having been sung, Jesus left the city along with his disciples and went to the nearby Mount of Olives, to a plot known as Gethsemane. There he bade the disciples wait and watch. He went a little further on, prostrated himself and prayed: "Father, if you will, let this cup pass me by; but not as I will, but as you will." Then he went back and found the disciples asleep, and said to them: "Why do you sleep? Get up and pray that I do not fall into temptation.[203] The spirit is willing, but the flesh is weak" (cf. Lk. 22:39–46). He had almost betrayed the voice that had proclaimed to him his election and divine sonship; but he had overcome the temptation to flee in the darkness of that night from Gethsemane, and somewhere to eke out an anonymous, secret existence. He submitted to the will of his Father in heaven to drink the cup, which he had already guessed was predestined for him.

Gethsemane.

Thereupon, the temple guard approached, augmented—according to John 18:3—by a Roman cohort, and Judas Iscariot with them. The latter came up to Jesus and kissed him so that the officers could identify him in the darkness. Someone struck out at the servant of the high priest and cut off his ear; but Jesus said: "Leave them alone!" Then he said to them: "Why have you come out against me with swords and clubs as against a brigand? I have been teaching daily in the temple and you never laid a finger on me." Then they all left him and fled, and Jesus was taken off to the high priest (cf. Lk. 22:47–53).

DEATH

In 62 A.D., the Sadducean high priest, Annas, convened a session of the Sanhedrin at which the Lord's brother James and other Christians were indicted before the judges, and condemned to be stoned. The Pharisees engineered the deposition of the high priest, for in their opinion, the session had been illegal—called without their knowledge.[204] The Sanhedrin was the Jewish supreme court and numbered seventy-one members. To pass sentence of death, the presence of twenty-three judges sufficed.[205] It may be assumed that the high priest had assembled a sufficient number, but all chosen from among his Sadducean friends who were the only ones to have been informed.

It has been pointed out earlier in this book that in the first three gospels the Pharisees are not mentioned in connection with the trial of Jesus; and it has also been suggested, on the basis of independent reports, that they could not have acquiesced in the surrender of Jesus to the Romans. If, then, there was a session of the Sanhedrin before the crucifixion of Jesus, it must have resembled very much the arbitrary assembly of distinguished Sadducees who condemned James, the Lord's brother, to death.

Was it an assembly of the Sanhedrin at all, that condemned Jesus to death? John knew nothing about it, and in the whole of Luke—not just in his description of the Passion—a verdict of the supreme court is not even mentioned.[206] Mark was the first to alter the ancient report; a session of the judiciary had to pass judgment. Then Matthew based his account upon Mark. According to Luke (22:66) the proceedings took place in the house of the high priest after that anguished night; in the morning Jesus was taken "to their Sanhedrin." According to Mark (14:53–65) and Matthew (26:57–68), the proceedings took place in the night itself; in the high priest's house "all the chief priests and the elders and the scribes were assembled" (Mk. 14:53; cf. Mt. 26:57). Later (Mk. 14:55; Mt. 26:59) the assembly suddenly

Tomb of the family of the Herods—with a rolling stone.

Entrance to the Tomb of the Kings.

becomes "the chief priests and the whole council." On the following morning—so writes Mark (15:1)—"the chief priests, with the elders and scribes, and the whole council held a consultation; and they bound Jesus and led him away and delivered him to Pilate." Matthew (27:1–2) omits "and the whole council," which he thought superfluous. Luke (22:26) and Matthew (26:59) explicitly mention the Sanhedrin only once; Mark mentions it twice (14:55; 15:1). Thus there are two possibilities. We may accept Luke's version, asking, however, on grounds of literary criticism, whether there was one or two sessions of the supreme court. Were, then, "the chief priests and the elders and scribes" who hurried to the high priest's house after the arrest of Jesus, really the Sanhedrin? They appeared earlier (Lk. 20:1) when, in the temple, they asked him about his authority to teach. The phrase used is thus a formal designation for the temple committee: the elders were the elders of the temple and the scribes were the temple secretaries.[207]

We can also deduce that it was not the Sanhedrin who condemned Jesus to death from the fact that he was buried at neither of the two graves reserved for those executed by order of this supreme council.[208] Joseph of Arimathea begged Pilate to let him have the body of Jesus. He took him down, wrapped him in linen, and laid him in a tomb cut out of the rock where no one had yet been laid (Lk. 23:50–56). This was a very special act of love, for in Palestine one can find scarcely any ancient Jewish graves that do not contain several occupants. Joseph of Arimathea was a member of the city council of Jerusalem—a rich man. Councillors were expected to dispense charity, as Joseph did over the burial of Jesus. According to John (19:39), Nicodemus, whom Jesus had met some time earlier, came too, bringing a mixture of myrrh and aloes, and together these two men buried Jesus. We know from rabbinic sources that Nicodemus' son, Gorion, was one of the Jerusalem councillors and one of the three richest patricians in the city. Later, during the Jewish-Roman war, the fanatical rebels burned down his granary.[209] Nicodemus probably died in the war, and his daughter then lived in dire poverty. Her marriage contract was signed by the peace-loving pupil of Hillel, Rabbi Jochanan ben Sakkai.[210] Nicodemus' son was most likely the Gorion who, at the beginning of the rising, took part in the action that led to the capitulation of the Roman garrison at Jerusalem.[211] Then, when the insurgents had forced all to take part in the war, a certain Joseph—son of Gorion—and Ananus the Sadducean high priest, who previously had had James the Lord's brother executed, and who was an opponent of the fanatics, were elected to supreme power in Jerusalem.[212] The father of this Joseph was almost certainly Gorion, a man of outstanding respectability and nobility, who was later executed in Jerusalem under the reign of terror of the fanatics.[213] Even earlier, a man named Gorion, son of Joseph, and the Pharisee, Simeon, son of Gamaliel who took the apostles' part and was St. Paul's teacher, had tried in vain to oppose the fanatics.[214] It would seem that all of these men belonged to the same propertied patrician families of Jerusalem, who had distinguished themselves by resistance to the extreme militant party of the fanatics, and who were close in outlook to the moderate Pharisees. St. John tells us that the councillor Nicodemus knew Jesus, and was able to take part in his burial. The fact that two Jerusalem councillors performed the final act of charity to Jesus proves that it would be false to think that the supreme authorities in Jewry had delivered Jesus up to the Romans.

When Jesus had been brought into the high priest's house, the chief of the temple leaders assembled there. At first they tried to find credible corroboration that Jesus had, in fact, uttered that dangerous saying about the destruction of the temple. At last they found two men who gave reliable evidence to the saying (Mt. 26:57–61). Then the high priest rose to his feet and said to Jesus: "You answer nothing?" and Jesus was silent. The public announcement of the destruction of the temple, which Jesus had probably made when he attacked the traders within the sanctuary, might well have seemed to the high priest sufficient reason for handing Jesus over to the Romans, because

The temple at Jerusalem, a reconstruction.

it was in the Romans' interest to protect holy places. Nevertheless, there were rumors that this Jesus was regarded as a Messiah,[215] and messianic movements were suppressed by the Romans, for the Messiah was truly the King of the Jews. To make even more certain of getting rid of this troublesome incendiary, the high priest said to Jesus, "If you are the Christ, tell us." Jesus replied: "From now on the Son of man shall be seated at the right hand of the power of God" (Lk. 22:69).

How could Jesus speak thus, for he must have known that he had come to the end of his life? The Old Testament had already recounted how both the prophet Elijah and Enoch never died,

121

but were taken up into heaven, and in Jesus' day this had caught the popular imagination. In those days, people believed the same about Moses, although the Bible did speak of his death. It was said of Melchizedek not only that he had neither father nor mother, but that he would appear as judge at the end of time;[216] people also believed that the prophet Jeremiah had never died.[217] We have seen, too, that there were men who were convinced that the beheaded John the Baptist had risen from the dead. According to the Revelation of St. John (11:3–12), two prophets will come, but "the beast that ascends from the bottomless pit will make war upon them and conquer them and kill them." Their bodies were to die in the streets of Jerusalem for three and a half days, and then they were to rise again and go up to heaven upon a cloud. Some twenty years after the death of Jesus, an Egyptian Jew appeared and asserted that he would liberate Jerusalem from the Romans; but the governor Felix marched against him with an army, and dispersed his band of supporters. The prophet himself vanished. The people believed that God was keeping him in hiding, and awaited his return. When St. Paul came to Jerusalem he was asked if he were the Egyptian.[218] There can be no doubt that the Crucified "appeared to Peter, then to the twelve. Then he appeared to more than five hundred brethren at one time, . . . Then he appeared to James, then to all the apostles." Last of all, he appeared to Paul on the road to Damascus (1 Cor. 15:3–8). When he answered the high priest's question about his Messiahship with the words, "From now on the Son of man shall be seated at the right hand of the power of God," did the man Jesus already believe that he, too, would escape the fate that threatened, or, as is more likely, that he would rise from the dead? At all events the high priest correctly understood that by these words Jesus was confessing that he was the Messiah. Therefore he said: "What need have we of further witnesses? You have heard it from his own mouth" (cf. Lk. 22:71).

After the court adjourned, the guards thought up a bit of amusement: they blindfolded Jesus and struck him, saying,

A Roman soldier.
From a relief.

"Prophesy! Who is it that struck you?" The Sadducees did not believe in angels or in the spirit of prophecy (Acts 23:8), and the officers of the high priest thought as their masters did. Next morning the leaders again met with the high priest, and only then did they finally decide to take the case to the Roman authorities. Jesus was taken before Pilate.

Stone pavement of the Antonia Fortress, where Pilate handed over Jesus for execution. The pavement is marked out for a game played by the Roman soldiers.

The Via Dolorosa.

The Roman governor asked Jesus: "Are you the King of the Jews?" The sources tell us that Jesus answered: "You have said it." That is really all that has been handed down to us. According to John (18:29–38), this ambiguous saying signifies a denial: "*You* say that I am a king." "Do you say this of your own accord, or did others say it to you about me?" In fact, perhaps Jesus made no answer at all to the Roman. Because Pilate had heard that Jesus was a Galilean, and therefore a subject of Herod, he sent the prisoner to Herod who was also up in Jerusalem for the Passover. The king questioned him thoroughly, but Jesus remained silent, and Herod sent him back to Pilate (Lk. 23:6–12).[219] The Fox, who had sought to take Jesus' life in Galilee, was able to see him in Jerusalem, where he confidently left him in the hands of the Roman governor, whose brutality was known far and wide.[220] The formalities of the case were now over. This courtesy on the part of Pilate led to the healing of the previous estrangement between Herod Antipas and Pilate.

Jesus shared imprisonment in the Roman fortress of the Antonia with at least three others. These were anti-Roman guerrillas, and chief among them was Barabbas. He had taken part in terrorism that had cost lives, and had been caught and imprisoned along with the others. The governor regarded it as his duty to crucify these terrorists—especially Barabbas. And if this were done on the great festival of the Jews, before the enormous pilgrim crowd, all would be bound to see the iron hand of Rome. The execution of a popular hero might lead to unrest, and the electric atmosphere of a pilgrim festival, especially the Passover, was always inclined to foment such unrest.[221] In all probability the Jewish "bandits" would have wanted to avenge Barabbas' death, and then the intractable Jewish people would have learned the feel of bare Roman swords. The hated high priests for their part must have feared that there would be a riot during the festival (Mt. 26:5). This could be avoided if Barabbas was kept alive.

An ideal opportunity presented itself. The Roman governor was in the habit of releasing a Jewish prisoner on the Passover. From rabbinic literature[222] we know that this amnesty often went by default, or was granted only after long weary entreaty. On this occasion, both the high priests and Pilate tried to turn it to their own advantage. Before the hearing in front of Pilate, the crowd had already gathered, and the people were clamoring for the customary clemency to a prisoner. Pilate seized the opportunity and said to them: "Do you want me to release for you the King of the Jews?" (Mk. 15:6–10). In this King of the Jews he saw little danger to the empire, and hoped that the Jews likewise would see that there was no sound reason for his

The Nile gods. Mosaic from Beth Shean. Inscription: Alexandria.

execution. If he let this man free, he could have Barabbas
crucified. Then the high priests intervened. The crowd did not
hate Jesus, but they loved Barabbas, the freedom-fighter. Thus
it was easy on this occasion for the high priests to appear on
the side of the populace whom they stirred up to demand the
release of Barabbas (Mk. 15:11). Then Pilate asked: "Then
what shall I do with the man whom you call the King of the
Jews?" The answer he got was: "Crucify him." According to
John (19:6) the cry came first of all from the high priests and
their henchmen.[223] In any case the acclamation was superfluous,

"Christ Presented to the People." Etching by Rembrandt.

for Pilate knew that if Barabbas went free, Jesus would be crucified. Once again Pilate tried his luck. He said that he could find
no charge against Jesus serious enough to justify execution. He
would scourge him and let him go (Lk. 23:22). Even that was
of no use; he had to let Barabbas go free; but Jesus·was scourged
and then handed over to be crucified (Mt. 27:26).

Apparently Jesus was handed over to Pilate without a verdict,
and nowhere in the sources is a verdict by Pilate reported. In

"Christ Presented to the People." Second version, 1655.

the catalogue of crimes of Pilate, provided by the philosopher, Philo of Alexandria,[224] among others we find "constant execution without passing judgment." It would seem, therefore, that Jesus' tragic end was preceded by no verdict of any earthly judiciary. It was the outcome of the grisly interplay of naked spheres of interest, in the shadow of brutal antagonisms, and to outward appearance, it had no real connection with the man Jesus and his cause. Only Rembrandt has been able to portray the dumb loneliness of Jesus at his trial—which was no trial. In an etching, he depicts Jesus as he is brought from Pilate out to the people, and hardly anybody is actually looking at this strange spectacle. Jesus is quite passive as though waiting until this senseless pantomime is over. This contrasts with the noisy hatred of the crowd in the gospels, but it is historically more correct. Apparently, Rembrandt was not satisfied with his portrayal, and so in a later version he removed the detached mob almost completely. Now an empty and horrid arch adorns the foreground of the scene. A single Jew remains on the right of the balcony, viewing the whole thing with pathetic and dreamlike intensity. "Who is it? A friend? A good man? Someone who sympathized? Someone who wanted to help? Was it one person only? Or were they all there? Was help at hand? Where was the High Court to which he had never penetrated?"[225] Now the Roman soldiers had to deal with Jesus. They led him into the interior of the hall of the Roman fortress and assembled the entire cohort. Then they dressed him in a purple cloak, plaited a crown of thorns, and placed it on his head. They put a reed in his right hand. When the mock king had received all his insignia, they genuflected and prostrated themselves before him—as before an oriental despot—and saluted him: "Hail, King of the Jews!" Then they spat on him, took away the reed, and struck him on the head with it (cf. Mk. 15:16–20). That was not the only time the heathen made fun of the Messianic hopes of the Jews. A few years after the death of Jesus, when the Jewish King Agrippa visited Alexandria the Alexandrians took a harmless imbecile called Karabas, "dragged the unfortunate man into the arena, raised him on high so that all could see him, put a crown of rushes on his head, dressed him in a straw cloak, and someone put a short stalk of the local papyrus in his hand in place of a scepter. Thus, like a stage clown he was given the insignia of a ruler and fitted out like a king; and youngsters hoisted sticks upon their shoulders like lances and acted the part of an armed guard. Others then came to do him obeisance or to seek justice or lodge a petition; finally the whole crowd shouted out 'Marin,'[226] for that was what a king was supposed to be called among the Syrians."[227] A badly preserved papyrus contains an account of a similar mocking of a comic king that took place also in Alexandria after the Jewish rising of 115–117 A.D. The Roman governor himself seems to have taken part in this.[228] The Jewish soldiers made grisly fun of Jesus. As earlier in the house of the high priest, the Sadducean officers had tormented Jesus in order to demonstrate the impotence of the Holy Spirit of prophecy, so now the Roman soldiers used the same prisoner to ridicule the Jewish hope of liberation.

Then the soldiers led Jesus away to be crucified. According to Roman law,[229] "instigators of a revolt or a riot or agitators of the people" were "either crucified or thrown to wild animals or banished to an island—according to their status." After Pilate, whose sense of justice was fairly unstable, had let Barabbas go free, he was obliged for good or ill to take the charge against Jesus more seriously than before. If he wished, he could have him crucified as an agitator of the people on account of the incident and the prophecy in the temple; and finally there were rumors that he was the Messiah. He had the words—upon which he had ironically played during the proceedings—written mockingly upon the cross: "King of the Jews."

Along the way, the Romans compelled a passing Jew called Simon from Cyrene[230] in North Africa to carry the cross of Jesus (Mk. 15:21). It was not uncommon for the Roman occupying forces to demand statute-labor from pilgrims on Jewish festivals.[231] The procession had left the city to go to Golgotha—the place of a skull. Compassionate Jews, as their custom was, offered Jesus wine mixed with myrrh to numb his death agony; but he refused it.[232] Then the three of them were crucified: two bandits, one on the right and one on the left, and Jesus in the middle, for he was indeed executed as "the King of the Jews." Jesus said: "Father, forgive them, for they know not what they do."[233] The soldiers divided up his clothing among them, and a sensation-loving mob stared at the execution. Some remarked ironically that he had said he would knock down the

A relief upon an ivory casket. C. 420–430 A.D.

temple and rebuild it. Let him try to come down from the cross! The high priests observed derisively: "He saved others, himself he cannot save—this King of Israel!"

The Roman soldiers, too, mocked him: they filled a sponge with vinegar, put it upon a reed, and pressed it against his lips. Even the two who were crucified alongside him reviled him. Then a cry was heard from the cross. Some of the bystanders thought he was calling upon Elijah. Others thought that he called out in despair: "My God, my God (Eli, Eli), why hast thou forsaken me?"[234] And Jesus died.

REFLECTIONS

PAUL

Therefore he had to be made like his brethren in every respect, so that he might become a merciful and faithful high priest in the service of God, to make expiation for the sins of the people. For because he himself has suffered and been tempted, he is able to help those who are tempted.

IMMANUEL KANT

In this portrayal we cannot fail to see the person who is not just the author of the religion that transcends mere dogma and is written in every heart (for this religion does not have an arbitrary origin) but is also the person who could evoke the veneration of the primitive, true Church . . . If the account appeals to ancient Mosaic legislation and preparation—as though these confirmed his claim—it does so not in support of the truth of the doctrines in question, but merely as an introduction to people who held completely and blindly to the old traditions.

JOHANN WOLFGANG VON GOETHE

> Jesus in silence His pure heart
> With thought of one sole God did fill;
> They who Himself to God convert
> Do outrage to His holy will

133

NOVALIS

The story of Christ is as much a *poem* as a history. For that matter, the only history that *is* history is the history that can also be fable.

GEORG BÜCHNER

The world contains only Epicureans—coarse and refined; and Christ was the most refined of them all.

HERMANN SAMUEL REIMARUS

It is, indeed, regrettable that Jesus did not confine himself entirely to the work of conversion, because he had such edifying and splendid things to say about this change of heart, and undoubtedly might have had much more to say to that effect. But conversion of heart was merely a preparation for his main purpose of erecting a kingdom. And this greatly detracts from the fine character which we would have been compelled to attribute to him on account of his sheer work of calling for a change of heart.

SOREN KIERKEGAARD

Thus it is incomprehensible—absolutely incomprehensible—for someone to be God and at the same time an individual man. He was truly God and hence God in such measure that he had entered the realm of unrecognizability, so that not flesh and blood, but their exact opposite enabled Peter to recognize him.

TOMÁŠ GARRIGUE MASARYK

Jesus does not strain transcendentalism; his religion is not specially designed for heaven but for earth and ordinary everyday life. He said little about the origin and the end of the world; he was not concerned with history, as was the Old Testament. The religion of Jesus is seen in morality and humanity; it is humanism *sub specie aeternitatis*.

FRIEDERICH NIETZSCHE

It is a pity that no Dostoyevski had lived close to this interesting *décadent*: I mean, someone who knew how to sense the overpowering charm of such a blend of the sublime, the pathological, and the childlike.

SIGMUND FREUD

The Jews had to bear the reproach from the new religious community, that they had murdered God. Unabridged, this reproach read thus: They refuse to admit that they murdered God, whereas we admit it and are thereby cleansed from its guilt. It then becomes easy to understand how much truth lies behind this reproach. The reason why the Jews have been unable to make the progress implied in admission that they murdered God would be the subject of special study. By this they have burdened themselves with tragic guilt; and they have been allowed to perform a very heavy penance for it.

RUDOLF STEINER

The personality of Jesus was capable of assuming into its own soul Christ the Logos, so that this became flesh in that personality. Since this assumption, the "I" of Jesus of Nazareth is Christ, and the exterior personality is bearer of the Logos. This event—the "I" of Jesus becoming Christ—is depicted in the baptism by John.

ALBERT SCHWEITZER

The reason why the Jesus of modern theology is so remarkably lifeless is this. Left within his eschatological world he is greater and operates—despite his distance—with greater elemental force than does the other Jesus. What Jesus accomplished was this: his natural morality took possession of late Judaistic eschatology and thus gave expression within the ideas of his time to the hopes and desires of an ethical world view.

CARL GUSTAV JUNG

The reality of evil and its inseparability from the good tear the antitheses apart and lead inexorably to crucifixion and the suspension of all that lives. Because the *anima* is *naturaliter christiana,* this consequence is bound to follow as inevitably as it did in the life of Jesus: we must all become "crucified with Christ," that is become suspended in a moral suffering that corresponds to the actual crucifixion. This imitation of Christ, when understood in the most profound sense, denotes a suffering which is far beyond what most people are able to bear.

136

MARTIN BUBER

All my life I have felt that Jesus was my elder brother. My own open brotherly relationship to him has become even stronger and purer, and today I can see him with surer and purer vision than before. I am more certain than ever that he merits a greater place in the history of Israel's faith, and that this place cannot be defined in terms of the usual categories.

OSWALD SPENGLER

Here is no philosophy. His sayings, which many of his companions remembered word for word until a ripe old age, are those of a child in the midst of an alien, spent, and sick world. Here is no social study, no set of problems, no meditation. He had the pure and unspoilt soul of a country without cities.

NOTES

1. On the view that Jesus' brothers and sisters were, in fact, his cousins, or children of Joseph by a previous marriage, see the excellent book by the Catholic scholar, J. Blinzler, *Die Brüder und Schwestern Jesu* (Stuttgart, 1967).

2. See Joel Carmichael, *Death of Jesus* (New York, 1962), pp. 59–66.

3. See Walter Bauer, *Das Leben Jesu im Zeitalter der neutestamentlichen Apokryphen* (Darmstadt, 1967), pp. 21–29. On the sonship of David, see A. Suhl, *Die Funktion der alttestamentlichen Zitate und Anspielungen im Markusevangelium* (Gütersloh, 1965), pp. 89–94; F. Hahn, *Christologische Hoheitstitel* (Göttingen, 1964), pp. 242–279.

4. See J. Liver, *The House of David . . . The Fall of the Second Commonwealth and After* (Jerusalem, 1959).

5. See Walter Bauer, *op. cit.,* p. 59.

6. On the chronology of Jesus, see Martin Dibelius, *From Tradition to Gospel* (New York, 1965); K. L. Schmidt, *Der Rahmen der Geschichte Jesu* (Darmstadt, 1964), pp. 1–17; Walter Bauer, *op. cit.,* pp. 279–310.

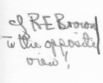 *of R. E. Brown / = the opposite / view!*

7. On the historical value of St. John's gospel, see C. H. Dodd, *Historical Tradition in the Fourth Gospel* (New York, 1963).

8. On Mark, see Willi Marxsen, *Der Evangelist Markus*[2] (Göttingen, 1959). On Luke, see Hans Conzelmann, *The Theology of St. Luke* (New York, 1961).

9. See Num. 18:15.

10. Mt. 21:23–27, and Lk. 20:1–8. See David Daube, *The New Testament and Rabbinic Judaism* (London, 1956).

11. F. Hahn, *op. cit.,* pp. 74–81.

12. *Ibid.,* pp. 75–76.

13. *Sayings of the Fathers* I:10.

14. Jacob Levy, *Wörterbuch über die Talmudim und Midraschim* III, (Berlin, 1924), p. 338.

15. Friedrich W. Nietzsche, *Antichrist*, para. 29, in *Complete Works*, 18 vols. (New York, 1964).

16. The expression which appears frequently in the gospels, comes from 1 Kgs. 17:18. See also Raymond E. Brown, *The Gospel According to John I–XII,* in *The Anchor Bible* series (New York, 1966), p. 99.

138

17. S. Pinès, "The Jewish Christians of the Early Centuries of Christianity According to a New Source," *The Israel Academy of Sciences and Humanities Proceedings,* II (Jerusalem, 1966), p. 61.

18. Vincent Taylor, *The Gospel According to St. Mark* (New York, 1966), pp. 235–236; see also K. L. Schmidt, *op. cit.,* pp. 122–123.

19. See E. Haenchen, *Die Apostelgeschichte*[2] (Göttingen, 1959); E. Meyer, *Ursprung und Anfänge des Christentums* (Stuttgart–Berlin, 1921–24), pp. 44–45.

20. 1 Cor. 15:7; Gal. 2:9; on the history of Jesus' family see Edgar Hennecke and W. Schneemelcher, *New Testament Apocrypha,* Vol. I, *Gospels and Related Writings* (Philadelphia, 1963).

21. Flavius Josephus, *Jewish Antiquities* XX, 9, 1, in *Complete Works* (Grand Rapids, Michigan, 1966).

22. Eusebius, *A History of the Church,* III, 11, 19–20, 32.

23. Lk. 2:35.

24. For bibliography, see Jean Steinmann, *Johannes der Täufer* (Hamburg, 1960); on John the Baptist and the Dead Sea scrolls, see William Brownlee, "John the Baptist in the Light of Ancient Scrolls," in Kr. Stendahl, ed., *The Scrolls and the New Testament* (New York, 1957); see also David Flusser, "The Baptism of John, and the Dead Sea Sect," in *Essays on the Dead Sea Scrolls* (Jerusalem, 1961), pp. 209–239.

25. *Canon of the Sect,* 8, 13–16; 9, 19–20.

26. Flavius Josephus, *Antiquities* XVIII, *op. cit.* 5, 2.

27. Mt. 14:3–12; Mk. 6:17–29; see Lk. 3:19–20.

28. *Canon of the Sect,* 5, 13–14.

29. Ibid., 3, 8–9.

30. Ibid., 3, 7–8.

31. Another opinion, dictated by apologetics, is to be found in Acts 19:1–7.

32. Lk. 3:21–22.

33. The Greek word translates the Hebrew "the only one." See C. H. Turner, "Ho Hyios mou ho agapetos" in *Journal of Theological Studies,* Vol. 27 (1926), pp. 113–129; see also, Morna D. Hooker, *Jesus and the Servant* (London, 1959), pp. 71, 183.

34. Joachim Jeremias, *Wörterbuch zum NT* V, p. 699; K. Stendahl, *The School of St. Matthew* (Uppsala, 1954), pp. 110, 144; David Flusser, "Blessed Are the Poor in Spirit," *op. cit.,* pp. 9–10 and note 25; F. Hahn, *op. cit.,* pp. 340–346.

35. Carl H. Kraeling, *John the Baptist* (New York, 1951), pp. 9–16;

E. Lohmeyer, *Das Urchristentum. Johannes der Täufer* (Göttingen, 1932), p. 26.

36. Mt. 8:14; Lk. 4:38.
37. Johannes Weiss in Schmidt, *op. cit.,* p. 34.
38. C. H. Dodd, *The Parables of the Kingdom* (Glasgow, 1961), p. 39, note 20.
39. I hope to discuss the temptations of Jesus by Satan in another work.
40. Mt. 11:2–6; Lk. 7:18–23.
41. Adolf von Harnack, *The Mission and Expansion of Christianity* I (Gloucester, Massachusetts).
42. Mt. 11:4–6; Lk. 7:22–23. The words "lepers are cleansed," and "the dead are raised up" are omitted because they do not occur in Jesus' source, Is. 29:18; 35:5; 61:1.
43. *The Assumption of Moses,* 10:1.
44. See Joachim Jeremias, *The Parables of Jesus* (New York, 1963), pp. 122–123.
45. Malachy 3:1.
46. H. L. Strack, and J. Billerbeck, *Kommentar zum Neuen Testament aus Talmud und Midrasch* (Munich, 1922–1961).
47. See *Aesop's Fables,* no. 37.
48. So it is, according to Matthew and Mark.
49. See Pinès, *op. cit.,* p. 63.
50. *Tossefta Berachoth* 5, 13; Billerbeck I, *op. cit.,* pp. 696–698.
51. *The Assumption of Moses,* chap. 7.
52. Num. 19:2.
53. Billerbeck I, *op. cit.,* p. 719. What is important is that Rabbi Johanan ben Sakkai had been speaking about a biblical commandment, whereas, the washing of hands was merely a late precept, and the purification precepts of the Pharisees were voluntary.
54. See also the important extra-canonical history of the clash between Jesus and the Pharisaical high priest in the forecourt of the temple in Joachim Jeremias, *Unknown Sayings of Jesus* (Naperville, Illinois, 1965), pp. 47–60.
55. Mechilta on Exodus 31:13 (103b); see W. Bacher, *Die Agada der Tannaiten* II (Strasburg, 1890), p. 493, note 2. See also, Vincent Taylor, *op. cit.,* pp. 218–220.
56. See J. N. Epstein, *Prolegomena ad litteras Tannaitieas* (Jerusalem, 1957), pp. 280–281 (in Hebrew).
57. See also Rudolf Bultmann, *History of the Synoptic Tradition* (New York, 1963), pp. 52 ff.
58. Literally, "the son of man"; see V. Taylor, *op. cit.,* p. 197.
59. In addition, see Paul Volz, *Der Geist Gottes* (Tübingen, 1910), p. 164.

60. See note 57.
61. *Autobiography* 12.
62. Phil. 3:5; Acts 23:6; 26:5.
63. *Autobiography,* 191.
64. Sota 22b.
65. Allusion to the story told in Num. 25:6–15.
66. *Damascus Book* 8, 12; 19, 25 (according to Ezek. 13:10).
67. *Hymnbook* 4, 6–8.
68. Sota 22b; *Berachoth* 14b.
69. So it is, according to *Berachoth* 14b.
70. Commentary on Nahum 2:7–10.
71. *Hymnbook* 4, 11.
72. As we see from Luke, the continuation (Mt. 23:34–36; Lk. 11:49–51) did not originally refer to the Pharisees.
73. Josephus, *Antiquities* II, 9, 1.
74. Justin, *Dialogue with Trypho,* chap. 47.
75. The words "till all shall have come to pass" do not seem to be words spoken by Jesus. On the meaning of these words see Billerbeck, *op. cit.,* pp. 143–144.
76. The word is usually translated "heathen," but, even in Jesus' mouth, it simply means "non-Jews," "Gentiles."
77. Here "Son of man" seems to mean "the man." Luke uses it of Jesus (22:27). It is significant that Luke as yet knows nothing of the Christological interpretation of the word with reference to the Passion of the Lord, which was introduced by Mark (Mk. 10:45b, and Mt. 20:28b).
78. On the whole question, see Joachim Jeremias, *Jesus' Promise to the Nations* (Naperville, Illinois, 1958).
79. See Pinès, *op. cit.*
80. *Sayings of the Fathers* 1, 3. See K. Schlesinger, *Die Gesetzeslehrer* (Berlin, 1934), p. 25. On what follows, see David Flusser, "The Two Ways of Justice, Judaism and Christianity," in *Harvard Theological Review.*
81. See also the legends in *Awoth de R. Nathan,* 5, 1, in Schlesinger, *op. cit.,* p. 25.
82. James B. Pritchard, ed., *Ancient Near Eastern Texts Relating to the Old Testament* (Princeton, 1955), p. 439.
83. Billerbeck II, *op. cit.,* p. 159.
84. Joma 8, 9; see R. Mayer, *Der Babylonische Talmud* (Munich, 1963).
85. *Sayings of the Fathers,* 2, 3; see R. Mayer, *op. cit.,* p. 328.
86. Billerbeck I, *op. cit.,* pp. 444–446.

87. It certainly was not first compiled from the Greek synoptic gospels; its Semitisms, among other things, prove this. *Polycarp* 2, 3, is dependent upon Clement as the introduction to the Lord's saying shows (1 *Clement* 13, 1b).

88. Billerbeck I, *op. cit.,* pp. 459–460. On Hillel's dictum in Shabbat 31a see Bacher I, *op. cit.,* p. 4.

89. *Slav Book of Enoch* 61, 1 (ed. Verleant), p. 59. See Billerbeck I, *op. cit.,* p. 460.

90. See Billerbeck I, *op. cit.,* p. 358. Earlier (p. 354) he argues against the assertion of modern Jewish scholars "that the old synagogue, even in New Testament times, had understood the command to love one's neighbor to be contained in the universal obligation to love others." Let us assume that he is right; but with what certainty may we conclude that Jesus specifically extended the command to love one's neighbor to embrace Gentiles?

91. *Awoth de R. Nathan* (second version), p. 53.

92. The phrase "and the prophets" was added later. We have tried to reconstruct the beginning of the Lord's saying according to the manner of speech of that time. The saying could be possible in its present form only if the enquirer had been wanting to discover whether Jesus knew the answer. Luke (10:25–28) spotted this difficulty and wanted to overcome it.

93. The saying does not come from Jesus: it has undergone Christian elaboration.

94. See note 90.

95. *Sayings of the Fathers,* 1, 3.

96. See note 68.

97. Sifre on Deut. 6:5. The correct text according to Midrash Tannaim on this passage.

98. See the *Book of Jubilees,* chap. 36; the Jewish "Two Ways," in the *Didache; Testament of Daniel,* 5, 3; *Testament of Issachar,* 5, 2; 7, 6; *Testament of Zabulun,* 5, 1. See also F. M. Braun, "Les Testaments des XII Patriarches" in *Revue Biblique* 67 (1960), pp. 531–532.

99. The phrase "or the prophets" does not seem to be original.

100. On the idiom see Rom. 3:31.

101. Baba Metzia, 58b.

102. *Loc. cit.*

103. Matthew abridges the saying, and Mark has elaborated it.

104. Midrash Haggadol on Ex. 20:14.

105. See J. P. Audet, "Affinités litteraires et doctrinales du Manuel de Discipline," in *Revue Biblique* (1952), pp. 219–238.

106. *Didache*, 3, 1–3.
107. Literally, "the Son of man."
108. *Negro Spirituals.*
109. *Canon of the Sect,* 5, 14–20.
110. *Damascus Book,* 6, 14–15.
111. As a rule, translated "through," because the word was not understood before the discovery of the scrolls. Linguistically this is impossible.
112. In the original, the Aramaic *mammona* (Hebrew, *mammon*) meaning a "possession."
113. *Canon of the Sect,* 1, 4–5.
114. See David Flusser, "Blessed are the Poor in Spirit," *op. cit.*
115. See Braun's article in note 98.
116. The text has, "for the Lord's sake." This is an interpolation from what follows.
117. Add special material in Lk. 14:14 (cf. perhaps, Lk. 16:31).
118. *Canon of the Sect,* 9, 21–26.
119. *Canon of the Sect,* 10, 17–20.
120. See especially Rom. 12:14; 13:7.
121. *Testament of Benjamin,* 4, 2–3; 5, 1; 5–7.
122. The end of the biblical saying is missing in Matthew, although it is precisely its closing words that Jesus explains.
123. Thus according to Lk. 6:30. Correct comment by G. Strecker, "Der Weg der Gerechtigkeit," *Untersuchung zur Theologie des Matthäus* (Göttingen, 1966), p. 134.
124. Instead of "as yourself," Matthew has: "and hate your enemy." There is no space here to reach a verdict about these words.
125. *Testament of Zabulun,* chap. 7.
126. See especially Joel Carmichael *op. cit.;* and see the discussion by W. G. Kümmel, "Jesusforschung seit 1950," in *Theologische Rundschau,* Vol. 31 (1966), pp. 312–313. The one saying of Jesus that can seriously be taken in an activist sense is Lk. 22:35–38, but Martin Dibelius, *op. cit.,* p. 200, seems to be right in saying, "An eschatological saying referring to the impending struggles and advising the purchase of a sword is interwoven into the dialogue, and prepares for the blow of the sword at the arrest."
127. See M. Hengel, *Die Zeloten,* Institutum Judaicum Tübingen (Leiden, 1961).
128. Acts 1:13; Mk. 3:18; Lk. 6:15.
129. M. Hengel, *op. cit.,* p. 384.
130. Targum on Zachariah 14:9.

131. Targum on Ezekiel 2:10.

132. Sifre on Deut. 32:29.

133. *Sayings of the Fathers,* 3, 6.

134. H. S. Horovitz and I. A. Rabban, eds. *Mechilta de Rabbi Nathan* (1960), pp. 150–151.

135. S. Schechter, ed., *Awoth de Rabbi Nathan* (1945), p. 72.

136. *Tossefta Sota,* 14, 4.

137. *Ketoboth,* 66b. See Bacher, *op. cit.,* vol. I, p. 42.

138. See *Assumption of Moses,* 10, 1–10; *Testament of Daniel,* 6, 1–5.

139. See Ph. Vielhauer, *Aufgätze zum Neuen Testament,* (Munich, 1965), p. vii.

140. Albert Schweitzer, *In Quest of the Historical Jesus* (New York, 1968), p. viii.

141. See Dr. Fr. Strauss, *Hermann Samuel Reimarus* (1862), pp. 182–185. Schweitzer, *op. cit.,* knew this book, but paid no attention to it.

142. See the quotation in "Testimonies."

143. L. Ragaz, *Die Botschaft vom Reiche Gottes* (1942), p. 280. See also *Die Geschichte der Sache Christi* (1945), pp. 112–113.

144. Joachim Jeremias: *The Parables of Jesus, op. cit.,* p. 227.

145. The explanation of Rabbi Akiba in support of the Messiahship of Bar Kochba is a different story.

146. *Hymnbook* 8, 4–14; 6, 15–16. See Betz, pp. 35–36.

147. Mt. 4:19.

148. See what L. Ragaz has to say in note 143.

149. Abba Hilkia and Rabbi Hanina bar Dossa.

150. See *Taanit,* 23; K. Schlesinger, *op. cit.,* pp. 71–77.

151. On the Jewish and early Christian custom of sending men out in pairs, see note 39.

152. *Taanit,* 24b.

153. *Berachot,* 34b.

154. *Taanit,* 23a; K. Schlesinger, *op. cit.,* pp. 62–65.

155. *Antiquities,* XIV, 2.

156. The so-called Josephus Goriondes (Josippon).

157. As is evident from Abba Hilkia whom we have cited, and from Mt. 23:7–9, and from other sources, in those days Abba, like Rabbi, was a title of honor.

158. *Taanit,* 23b.

159. Joachim Jeremias, "Abba," *Studien zur neutestamentlichen Theologie und Zeitgeschichte* (Göttingen, 1966), pp. 15–67, and Ven Iersel correctly perceived that, among the rabbis, addressing God as "our Father" did not have the same weight as "my

Father" or "Abba" as used by Jesus. Jeremias could not find "Abba" used to address God in Talmudic literature; but considering the scarcity of rabbinic material on charismatic prayer, this does not tell us very much.

160. Thus according to Lk. 10:22. On the meaning see G. Dalman, *Die Worte Jesu* (Leipzig, 1930), pp. 231–233.

161. The continuation of the saying (Mt. 11:28–30) also seems to be original.

162. E. Meyer, *op. cit.* I, pp. 280–291, correctly guessed that there were such hymns in ancient Judaism.

163. *Hymnbook,* 2, 9–10.

164. "Beloved" is the Greek translation of "only": see note 33.

165. E. Meyer, *op. cit.,* I, pp. 151–157.

166. See Is. 5:1–7. At the beginning of the parable Jesus alludes to this prophetic utterance.

167. Sifre on Deut. 32:9. See Billerbeck, *op. cit.,* I, p. 874.

168. On this see Morna Hooker, *op. cit.*

169. This concept is widespread in scientific literature, and also among the faithful. The abstruse concepts to which it can lead, if taken seriously, is shown in H. J. Schonfield's book, *The Passover Plot* (New York, 1966).

170. I regard the continuation (Mt. 16:18–19) also as fundamentally genuine. See David Flusser, "Qumran und die Zwölf" in *Initiation* (Leiden, 1965), pp. 138–139.

171. The belief concerning Elijah was based upon Malachy, and that concerning Moses was based on Deuteronomy 18. See F. Hahn, *op. cit.,* pp. 351–404.

172. See David Flusser's article, *"Antijudaismus im Neuen Testament?"*, in W. P. Eckert, N. P. Levinson and Martin Stöhr, eds., *Exigetische und systematische Beiträge* (Munich, 1967), p. 67.

173. Rudolf Bultmann, *Theology of the New Testament* (New York, 1951), pp. 30f. On the question of Jesus' awareness of his Messiahship, see *op. cit.,* pp. 26–32.

174. See note 107.

175. For example, *Ethiopian Book of Enoch,* 48, 10; 52, 4.

176. *Ibid.,* chap. 71.

177. J. A. Robinson, ed., *The Testament of Abraham* (1892), chaps. 12–13, pp. 90, 92.

178. See M. de Jonge and A. S. Van der Woude, "11 Q Melchizedek and the New Testament" in *New Testament Studies* (1966), pp. 301–321; see also David Flusser, "Melchizedek" in *Christian*

News from Israel (1966) pp. 23–29. Obviously, this Essene fragment is important in connection with Hebrews.

179. Mk. 15:26.

180. Mt. 26:64 adds "you have said"; Mk. 14:62 adds "I am he"; Lk. 22:67–70 adds, among other things, "you say that I am."

181. See Leo van Puyvelde, *L'Agneau mystique d'Hubert et Jean van Eyck* (1964), p. 30.

182. Lk. 22:15.

183. See S. Safrai, *Pilgrimage at the Time of the Second Temple* (Tel Aviv, 1965), p. 132, who quotes also the Midrash on Psalm 118 (Baber, ed., p. 488). The people of Jerusalem used to say: "Save us O Lord! (Hosanna!)," and the pilgrims replied: "So be it, Lord!" The people of Jerusalem used to say: "Blessed is he who comes in his name!" and the pilgrims replied: "We bless you from the house of the Lord."

184. According to John 12:13, Jesus was welcomed with palm branches also. Mt. 21:8 and Mk. 11:8 are different. Luke omits this.

185. See S. Safrai, *op. cit.,* p. 133.

186. Mk. 11:18–19; Lk. 19:47–48. The scribes, missing in a few of the manuscripts of Luke, may have been the temple scribes.

187. Flavius Josephus, *The Wars of the Jews,* VI, 5, 3 (Baltimore, 1959).

188. See S. Safrai, *op. cit.,* pp. 147–149.

189. Is. 56:7.

190. Jer. 7:11.

191. That which certainly belongs to the ancient account can be read in Luke. Mk. 11:15–17 expands the account on the basis of hearsay. We cannot tell, therefore, whether or not Jesus succeeded in overturning some of the tables of the merchants. Mt. 21:12–12 follows Mark, but turns Jesus' attempt to drive out the merchants into an accomplished deed. Jn. 2:13–17 transposes the incident to the beginning of Jesus' public life, and he underlines and exaggerates the episode. However, he does preserve the connection between the cleansing of the temple and the prophecy about the temple (2:19).

192. According to the original text of Mt. 26:60, the two who inform the high priest of the saying are not false witnesses. The saying is missing from Luke.

193. As in Mt. 23:24 and, perhaps, Mt. 23:37.

194. See Rudolf Bultmann, *History of the Synoptic Tradition, op. cit.,* pp. 125 f., and in *Supplement,* p. 403. See also David Flusser, "Two Notes on the Midrash on 2 Samuel VII, 1. The Temple Not

Made with Hands in the Qumran Doctrine" in *Israel Exploration Journal* (1959) pp. 99–104.

195. See note 191.

196. Mt. 26:17–20. See S. Safrai, *op. cit.*, pp. 133–134.

197. Lk. 22:15 reads: "before I suffer."

198. Thus in an important manuscript.

199. It is more likely that in both sayings Jesus said: "in the world to come."

200. Cf. Lk. 22:15–19. In the important manuscript mentioned in note 198, this is where the text ends. On this point see R. Otto, *Sünde und Unschuld* (Munich, 1932), pp. 96–122.

201. Mk. 14:27.

202. Lk. 22:34.

203. In the sources: "that you do not fall into temptation." See Jean Hering: "Zwei exegetische Probleme in der Perikope von Jesus in Gethsemane," in *Supplementum in NT* (1962), pp. 64–69.

204. Flavius Josephus, *Antiquities* XX, *op. cit.*, 9, 1.

205. Mishna Sanhedrin, 4, 1.

206. See Paul Winter, *On the Trial of Jesus* (Berlin, 1961), p. 28. Quite clearly Luke himself meant that the Jews would have condemned Jesus to death (Acts 13:27).

207. An edict of Antiochus III to the Jews in 198 B.C. said: "let the senate and the priests, and the scribes of the temple, and the sacred singers, be discharged from poll-money and the crown tax, and other taxes also" (Flavius Josesphus, *Antiquities* XII, 3, 3).

208. Mishna Sanhedrin, 6, 5. See Billerbeck I, *op. cit.*, p. 1049.

209. Gittin 56a.

210. Kethuboth 66b.

211. Flavius Josephus, *Wars of the Jews*, II, 13, 5; *Antiquities* XX,

212. *Ibid.* II, 22, 1.

213. *Ibid.* IV, 6, 1.

214. *Ibid.*, IV, 3, 9.

215. For all of this see *Wars of the Jews*, in various places.

216. See David Flusser, *Melchizedek*, op. cit.

217. Mt. 16:14. See also R. Harris, *The Rest of the Words of Baruch* (1889).

218. Flavius Josephus, *Wars of the Jews*, II, 13, 5; *Antiquities* XX, 8, 6; Acts 21:38. See M. Hengel, *op. cit.*, pp. 236–237.

219. The account is historical, as Acts 4:25–28 proves. There we find a typological interpretation of Psalm 2:1–2 in the spirit of an Essene commentary; and there, Herod's complicity with Pilate in

the death of Jesus is mentioned. The Jewish-Christian texts in Pinès, *op. cit.,* pp. 55–56, and the apocryphal Gospel of Peter, report the same things.

220. On Pilate see E. Schürer, *Geschichte des jüdischen Volkes im Zeitalter Jesu* I (Leipzig, 1901), pp. 488–492. In a work of the Jewish philosopher, Philo of Alexandria (*Legatio ad Gaium,* 299–305) there is a letter of the Jewish King Agrippa to Emperor Caligula, which Philo had presumably drafted for the king. This letter says of Pilate that he was "by nature inflexible, self-willed and hard." The crimes of his administration were listed as: "bribery, tyranny, pillage, violence, calumny, constant execution without passing of verdict, and endless, insufferable cruelty" (302). It may be no accident that the list of crimes adds up to seven.

221. See S. Safrai, *op. cit.,* p. 159.

222. *Ibid.,* pp. 159–160.

223. This important narrative in John is generally overlooked. The high priests and their servants were thus the organized popular mood of those days. According to the ancient account, the shout "Crucify!" rang out twice (Mk. 15:13, 14). This is intrinsically possible. The fact that the various gospels have intensified the shout can be proved by everyone for himself. The fact that the supposed *Deicidium* led to a concrete *homicidium* belongs to a later period.

224. See note 220.

225. Franz Kafka, *The Trial* (New York), p. 248.

226. "Marin" is another Aramaic form of "Maran" (1 Cor. 16:22), meaning "Lord."

227. Philo, *In Flaccum,* 36–39. See Philo of Alexandria, *On Proofs of God's Power* (Cambridge, Massachusetts).

228. Text in V. A. Tcherikover and A. Fuks, eds., *Corpus Papyrorum Judaicarum* II (Cambridge, Massachusetts, 1960), pp. 61–62.

229. Paulus, sent. 5, 22, 1 = dig. 48, 19, 38, par. 2. See V. Betz, *Was wissen wir von Jesus* (Stuttgart–Berlin, 1965), pp. 56–57; M. Hengel, *op. cit.,* pp. 33–34.

230. In those days, Cyrene was an important Jewish center. The name Simon and those of his sons Alexander and Rufus, were very common among Jews everywhere. Simon is the equivalent of the biblical Simeon; Rufus is the equivalent of the biblical name Reuben. See *Corpus Papyrorum Judaicarum* I, *op. cit.* (1957), p. 29.

231. See S. Safrai, *op. cit.,* p. 159.

232. Mk. 15:23; see J. Billerbeck I, *op. cit.,* pp. 1037–1038.
233. Lk. 23:24. The saying has an authentic ring about it, but after the second century was often omitted by transcribers who knew well what they were doing.
234. This quotation from Psalm 22:2 occurs in Mk. 15:34 and in Mt. 27:46 as Jesus' last words. It seems to us to be a less kindly interpretation by the crowd of Jesus' last cry, than that he was calling upon Elijah. That there is a "true" and a "false" interpretation itself shows that the saying is uncertain.

CHRONOLOGICAL TABLE

	made himself high priest and king after his mother's death. Start of the civil war. Hyrcanus was supported by the Pharisees, Aristobolus by the Sadducees.
65 (early)	Aristobolus besieged in the temple mount by Hyrcanus and his Arabian allies. Honi (Onias) the drawer of circles killed.
64	The Roman general Pompey brought the Syrian Empire of the Seleucids to an end.
63	Pompey in Damascus in early part of year. He arbitrated between the two brothers and decided in favor of Hyrcanus; he imprisoned Aristobolus and conquered Jerusalem in autumn. Judea became a vassal principality of Rome with Hyrcanus II as high priest and president. Catiline's conspiracy put down in Rome.
47	The Idumean Antipater, father of Herod, installed by Caesar as governor of Judea.
44	Caesar assassinated.
43	Antipater assassinated.
40	Hyrcanus II deposed by the Parthians who were led by his nephew Antigonus; exiled to Babylon, and executed by Herod in 30 B.C.
37	Antigonus defeated by the Romans and Herod installed by Anthony as King of Judea (37–4 B.C.).
31	Octavian (late Augustus) defeated Anthony at Actium.
31 B.C.— 14 A.D.	Caesar Augustus.
c. 20 B.C.— 40 A.D.	The Jewish philosopher Philo of Alexandria.
c. 20 B.C.	The two great Pharisee scribes Hillel and Shammai.
4 B.C.	Death of Herod the Great. Division of the empire among his sons: Archelaus, Ethnarch of Judea, Samaria and Johunea (4 B.C.—6 A.D.); Herod Antipas, Tetrarch of Galilee and Perea (4 B.C.—39 A.D.); Philip, husband of Salome, Tetrarch of the northeast (4 B.C.—34 A.D.).
c. 2	The birth of Jesus.
A.D.	
6	Banishment of Archelaus. Judea under Roman governors. The Zealot (fanatics) movement founded by Judas the Galilean.

6–15	Annas (Ananos) the Sadducee, father-in-law of Caiaphas, high priest.
14–37	Tiberias Caesar.
c. 18–37	Caiaphas, son-in-law of Annas, high priest. He handed Jesus over to Pilate.
26–36	Pontius Pilate governor of Judea.
28/9	John the Baptist appeared. Baptism of Jesus and beginning of his ministry.
30 (Easter)	Crucifixion of Jesus.
c. 30	The scribe Gamaliel, teacher of St. Paul.
c. 35	Martyrdom of Stephen in Jerusalem.
37–41	Gaius Caligula Caesar.
c. 37–100	The Jewish historian Flavius Josephus.
39	Deposition of Herod Antipas.
41–44	Agrippa I, King of the Jews.
41–54	Claudius Caesar.
44	Judea again under Roman governors.
50–100	Agrippa II, Ethnarch; from 53, king of part of northern Palestine.
54–68	Nero Caesar.
62	Annas (Ananos) II, son of Annas I and grandson of Caiaphas, high priest. He had James the brother of the Lord executed.
64	Fire in Rome. Persecution of Christians. Paul and Peter executed in Rome.
66	Insurrection broke out in Palestine.
68–69	Caesars: Galba, Otto, Vitellius, and finally Vespasian (69–70).
70	Conquest of Jerusalem and destruction of the temple by Titus, son of Vespasian.

BIBLIOGRAPHY

1. History and Ancient Jewish Writings

W. BACHER. *Die Agada der Tannaiten* (Strassburg: I, 1903; II, 1890).

H. L. STRACK and J. BILLERBECK. *Kommentar zum Neuen Testament aus Talmud und Midrasch* (Munich, 1922–1961).

B. GERHARDSSON. *Memory and Manuscript*[2] (Uppsala, 1964).

M. HENGEL. *Die Zeloten* (Leiden, 1961).

JOACHIM JEREMIAS. *Jerusalem zur Zeit Jesu*[3] (Göttingen, 1962).

FLAVIUS JOSEPHUS. *Antiquities of the Jews,* in *Complete Works* (Grand Rapids, 1963).

———. *The Jewish Wars* (Baltimore, 1959).

E. KAUTZSCH. *Die Apokryphen und Pseudepigraphen des Alten Testaments* (Tübingen, 1900).

Kontexte, Vol. III, "Die Zeit Jesu" (Stuttgart–Berlin, 1966).

D. HANNS LILJE. *Die Lehre der zwölf Apostel* (Hamburg, 1955).

J. LIVER. *The House of David . . . to the Fall of the Second Commonwealth and After* (Jerusalem, 1959) [Hebrew].

E. LOHSE. *Die Texte aus Qumran, hebräisch und deutsch* (Darmstadt, 1964).

J. MAIER. *Die Texte vom Toten Meer* (Munich–Basel, 1960).

S. MOWINKEL. *He That Cometh* (Oxford, 1956).

PHILO OF ALEXANDRIA. *On Proofs of God's Power* (Cambridge, Massachusetts, no date).

JAMES B. PRITCHARD, ed. *Ancient Near Eastern Texts Relating to the Old Testament* (Princeton, 1955).

P. RIESSLER. *Altjüdisches Schrifttum ausserhalb der Bibel* (Augsburg, 1928).

S. SAFRAI. *Pilgrimage at the Time of the Second Temple* (Tel Aviv, 1965) [Hebrew].

K. SCHLESINGER. *Die Gesetzeslehrer* (Berlin, 1934).

K. SCHUBERT. *Die Gemeinde vom Toten Meer* (Munich, 1958).

E. SCHÜRER. *Geschichte des jüdischen Volkes im Zeitalter Jesu,* 3 vols. (Leipzig, 1901, 1907, 1909).

E. SJÖBERG. *Der Menschensohn in dem äthiopischen Henochbuch* (Lund, 1946).

P. VOLZ. *Die Eschatologie der jüdischen Gemeinde im neutestamentlichen Zeitalter* (Tübingen, 1934).

2. The Gospel

A. J. BELLINZONI. "The Sayings of Jesus in the Writings of Justin the Martyr," in *Nov. Test. Spl.* XVII (1967).

RAYMOND E. BROWN. *The Gospel According to John, I—XIII,* The Anchor Bible series (New York, 1966).

RUDOLF BULTMANN. *History of the Synoptic Tradition* (New York, (1963).

W. BUSSMANN. *Synoptische Studien,* Vols. I—III (Halle, 1925–1931).

HANS CONZELMANN. *The Theology of St. Luke* (New York, 1961).

MARTIN DIBELIUS. *From Tradition to Gospel* (New York, 1965).

C. H. DODD. *Historical Tradition in the Fourth Gospel* (Cambridge, 1963).

W. F. FARMER. *The Synoptic Problem* (New York, 1964).

ADOLF VON HARNACK. *Sprüche und Reden Jesu: Die zweite Quelle des Matthäus und Lukas* (Leipzig, 1907).

EDGAR HENNECKE and W. SCHNEEMELCHER. *New Testament Apocrypha,* 2 vols. (Philadelphia, 1963 and 1966).

EDWIN HOSKYNS and F. NOEL DAVEY, *Riddle of the New Testament* (Naperville, Illinois, 1958).

R. HUMMEL. *Die Auseinandersetzung zwischen Kirche und Judentum im Matthäusevangelium²* (Munich, 1966).

JOACHIM JEREMIAS. *Unknown Sayings of Jesus* (Naperville, Illinois, 1965).

G. D. KILPATRICK. *The Origins of the Gospel According to St. Matthew²* (Oxford, 1950).

E. KLOSTERMANN. *Das Markusevangelium,* HNT⁴ (Tübingen, 1950).

———. *Das Matthäusevangelium,* HNT² (Tübingen, 1927).

———. *Das Lukasevangelium,* HNT² (Tübingen, 1929).

R. L. LINDSEY. "A Modified Two-Document Theory of the Synoptic . . . Interdependence," in *Novum Testamentum,* Vol. VI (1963), pp. 239–263.

E. LOHMEYER. *Das Evangelium des Markus* (Göttingen, 1963).

———. *Das Evangelium des Matthäus* (Göttingen, 1962).

WILLI MARXSEN. *Der Evangelist Markus²* (Göttingen, 1959).

A. RESCH. *Agrapha* (Darmstadt, 1967).

A. SCHLATTER. *Der Evangelist Matthäus⁵* (Stuttgart, 1959).

———. *Das Evangelium des Lukas²* (Stuttgart, 1960).

K. L. SCHMIDT. *Der Rahmen der Geschichte Jesu* (Berlin, 1919; Neudruck: Darmstadt, 1964).

KR. STENDAHL. *The School of St. Matthew* (Uppsala, 1954).

G. STRECKER. *Der Weg der Gerechtigkeit: Untersuchung zur Theologie des Matthäus* (Göttingen, 1966).

A. SUHL. *Die Funktion der alttestamentlichen Zitate und Anspielungen im Markusevangelium* (Gütersloh, 1965).

VINCENT TAYLOR. *The Gospel According to St. Mark* (New York, 1966).

L. VAGANAY. *Le problème synoptique* (Paris, 1954).

3. Jesus

LEO BAECK. "Paulus, die Pharisäer und das Neue Testament," in *Das Evangelium als Urkunde der jüdischen Glaubensgeschichte* (Frankfurt, 1961).

WALTER BAUER. *Das Leben Jesu im Zeitalter der neutestamentlichen Apokryphen* (Tübingen, 1909; Neudruck: Darmstadt, 1967).

SCH. BEN CHORIN. *Bruder Jesus. Der Nazarener in jüdischer Sicht* (Munich, 1967).

V. BETZ. *Was wissen wir von Jesus* (Stuttgart–Berlin, 1965).

J. BLINZER. *Die Brüder und Schwestern Jesu* (Stuttgart, 1967).

————. *Der Prozess Jesu* (Regensburg, 1955).

G. BORNKAMM. *Jesus von Nazareth* (Stuttgart, 1965).

WILLIAM H. BROWNLEE. "John the Baptist in the New Light of Ancient Scrolls," in Kr. Stendahl, ed., *The Scrolls and the New Testament* (New York, 1957).

RUDOLF BULTMANN. *Jesus* (Hamburg, 1967).

JOEL CARMICHAEL. *Death of Jesus* (New York, 1962).

G. DALMAN. *Jesus-Jeschua* (Leipzig, 1922).

————. *Orte und Wege Jesu* (Gütersloh, 1924).

————. *Die Worte Jesu* (Leipzig, 1930).

W. D. Davies. *The Setting of the Sermon on the Mount* (Cambridge, 1964).

MARTIN DIBELIUS. *Jesus* (Berlin, 1949).

CHARLES H. DODD. *The Parables of the Kingdom* (Glasgow, 1961).

A. FINKEL. *The Pharisees and the Teacher of Nazareth* (Leiden, 1964).

DAVID FLUSSER. "The Baptism of John, and the Dead Sea Scrolls," in *Essays on the Dead Sea Scrolls* (Jerusalem, 1962), pp. 209–239 [Hebrew].

————. "Blessed Are the Poor in Spirit," in *Israel Exploration Journal* (1960), pp. 1–12.

————. "Die konsequente Philologie und die Worte Jesu," in *Almanach für das Jahr des Herrn 1963* (Hamburg, 1963).

————. "Qumran und die Zwölf," in *Initiation* (Leiden, 1965), pp. 134–146.

F. HAHN. *Christologische Hoheitstitel* (Göttingen, 1964).

MORNA D. HOOKER. *Jesus and the Servant* (London, 1959).

B. M. F. VAN IERSEL. "Der Sohn," *Nov. Test. Suppl.* III (Leiden, 1961).

JOACHIM JEREMIAS. *The Parables of Jesus* (New York, 1963).

————. *Jesus' Promise to the Nations* (Naperville, Illinois, 1958).

A. JÜLICHER. *Die Gleichnisse Jesu* (Tübingen, 1910; Darmstadt, 1963).

E. KÄSEMANN. "Das Problem des historischen Jesus," in *Exegetische Versuche und Besinnungen. Gesammelte Aufsätze,* Vol. I (Göttingen, 1960) pp. 187–214.

CARL H. KRAELING. *John the Baptist* (New York, 1951).

W. G. KÜMMEL. *Verheissung und Erfüllung* (Zürich, 1956).

XAVIER LÉON-DUFOUR. *Les évangiles et l'histoire de Jésus* (Paris, 1963).

E. LOHMEYER. *Das Urchristentum: Johannes der Täufer* (Göttingen, 1932).

R. OTTO. *Reich Gottes und Menschensohn*[3] (1954).

HUGH J. SCHONFIELD. *The Passover Plot* (New York, 1966).

ALBERT SCHWEITZER. *Geschichte der Leben-Jesu-Forschung*[6] (Tübingen, 1951).

E. STAUFFER. *Jesus, Gestalt und Geschichte* (Bern, 1957).

JEAN STEINMANN. *Johannes der Taüfer* (Hamburg, 1960).

H. E. TÖDT. *Der Menschensohn in der synoptischen Überlieferung* (Gütersloh, 1959).

PAUL WINTER. *On the Trial of Jesus* (Berlin, 1961).

W. WREDE. *Das Messiasgeheimnis in den Evangelien*[3] (Göttingen, 1963).

4. The New Testament

MARTIN BUBER. *Zwei Glaubensweisen* (Zürich, 1950).

RUDOLF BULTMANN. *Die Theologie des Neuen Testaments* (Tübingen, 1958).

MARC-ALAIN CHEVALLIER. *L'Esprit et le Messie dans le Bas-Judaisme et le Nouveau Testament* (Paris, 1958).

DAVID DAUBE. *The New Testament and Rabbinic Judaism* (London, 1956).

J. W. DOEVE. *Jewish Hermeneutics in the Synoptic Gospels and Acts* (Te Assen, 1953).

FEINE-BEHM-KÜMMEL. *Einleitung in das Neue Testament*[13] (Heidelberg, 1964).

DAVID FLUSSER. "Antijudais im Neuen Testament?" in W. P. Eckert, N. P. Levinson, and Martin Stöhr, eds., *Exegetische und systematische Beiträge* (Munich, 1967).

————. "The Dead Sea Sect and Pre-Pauline Christianity," in *Aspects of the Dead Sea Scrolls, Scripta Hierosolymitana* IV (Jerusalem, 1958), pp. 215–266.

————. "Melchizedek and the Son of Man," in *Christian News from Israel* (1966), pp. 23–29.

————. "The Two Ways of Justice, Judaism and Christianity," in *Harvard Theological Review*.

————. "Two Notes on the Midrash on 2 Samuel VII, 1: The Temple Not Made with Hands in the Qumran Doctrine," in *Israel Exploration Journal* (1959), pp. 99–104.

L. GOPPELT. *Christentum und Judentum im ersten und zweiten Jahrhundert* (Gütersloh, 1954).

E. HAENCHEN. *Die Apostelgeschichte*[2], (Göttingen, 1959).

ADOLPH VON HARNACK. *The Mission and Expansion of Christianity,* Vol. I (Gloucester, Massachusetts, no date).

JOACHIM JEREMIAS. *Abba: Studien zur neutestamentlichen Theologie und Zeitgeschichte* (Göttingen, 1966).

M. DE JONGE AND A. S. VAN DER WOUDE. "11Q Melchizedek and the New Testament," in *New Testament Studies* (1966), pp. 301–326.

E. LOHSE. *Märtyrer und Gottesknecht* (Göttingen, 1955).

E. MEYER. *Ursprung und Anfänge des Christentums* (Stuttgart–Berlin, 1921–1924).

ST. NEILL. *The Interpretation of the New Testament, 1861–1961* (Oxford, 1966).

R. OTTO. *Sünde und Urschuld* (Munich, 1932).

S. PINÈS. "The Jewish Christians of the Early Centuries of Christianity According to a New Source," in *The Israel Academy of Sciences and Humanities Proceedings,* Vol. II, no. 13 (Jerusalem, 1966).

PH. VIELHAUER. *Aufsätze zum Neuen Testament* (Munich, 1965).

INDEX OF NAMES

158